PSYCHOLOGY and ENVIRONMENT

PSYCHOLOGY and ENVIRONMENT

Translated by David Canter and Ian Griffiths

Claude Levy-Leboyer

SAGE PUBLICATIONS
Beverly Hills / London / New Delhi

Translated from the French by David Canter and Ian Griffiths

English edition, Copyright © 1982 by Sage Publications, Inc.

Original French edition, *Psychologie et environment,* Copyright © 1979 by Presses Universitaires de France

For information address:

SAGE Publications, Inc.
275 South Beverly Drive
Beverly Hills, California 90212

SAGE Publications India Pvt. Ltd.
C-236 Defence Colony
New Delhi 110 024, India

SAGE Publications Ltd.
28 Banner Street
London EC1Y 8QE, England

Printed in the United States of America

Library of Congress Cataloging in Publication Data

Levy-Leboyer, Claude.
   Psychology and environment.

   Translation of: Psychologie et environnement.
   Bibliography: p.
   1. Environmental psychology. I. Title.
BF353.L4813   155.9   81-21382
ISBN 0-8039-1789-9 (cloth)   AACR2
ISBN 0-8039-1790-2 (pbk.)

SECOND PRINTING, 1984

Contents

Introduction

The environment is a recent concern, but nonetheless a major one. For many years, the word "ecology" only meant something to white-coated scientists, not to the majority of people. Today, however, ecology is a political issue as well as an important field of research. The applied human sciences have not escaped this trend. Their traditional aim of helping man to adapt to his environment now has the complementary aim of helping people to construct a habitat which meets their needs. What role can psychology play in this? What facts have already been established and how can they be described and used? What are the obstacles in the way of scientific progress in this new field? What is the future of this new application of psychology? What is the relation between environmental psychology and its parent disciplines, general and applied psychology?

This slim volume attempts to answer these questions by reviewing research in the field of environmental psychology. A very large proportion of these studies come from the United States. This should come as no surprise, because the high level of development in the applied social sciences in the United States is associated with rapid population growth, industrialization, and urbanization. However, psychological investigation of the environment has also had significant development in Europe, particularly in Great Britain and Sweden, and, more recently, in France.

At the beginning of the 1960s, environmental psychology took root simultaneously in three different places. Ittelson and

Proshansky began their study of the influence of hospital architecture on the behavior of mental patients in New York in 1958. At about the same time, Paul Sivadon, in France, with the support of the World Health Organization, became interested in the influence of the physical environment upon the therapeutic process in mental patients. In 1964, Kevin Lynch and his students at the Massachusetts Institute of Technology analyzed the perception of urban space and drew attention to this topic by publishing the now classic *Image of the City*.

In the following decade, two volumes emphasized the importance for psychologists, architects, and planners of the psychological problems raised by urban planning: Edward T. Hall's *The Hidden Dimension* (1966) and Robert Sommer's *Personal Space* (1969). Finally, the new discipline acquired scientific status and came of age with the appearance of three publications: a special issue of the *Journal of Social Issues* (1966), an article in the *American Psychologist* by Wohlwill, and Kenneth Craik's article in the 1973 *Annual Review of Psychology*.

Even if a reviewer were to concentrate on the major works, there has been far too much published in the last ten years for the task to be easy. Contrast, for example, the bibliography of Daniel Stokols's article in the 1978 *Annual Review*, which appeared only five years later than Craik's. The first textbook on environmental psychology appeared, written by Ittelson et al. in 1974, and the journal, *Environment & Behaviour*, had been appearing from 1960 onwards. University research groups in environmental psychology had also begun to multiply, not only in the United States (notably at the City University of New York and the University of California both at Irvine and at Berkeley), but also in Europe (at the Universities of Surrey, England; Strasbourg, France; and Lund, Sweden) and Canada (British Columbia, Vancouver). International conferences for architects and psychologists have been held every year under the aegis of EDRA (Environmental Design Research Association), the proceedings of which are published, and attendance has exhibited a steady growth. Finally, the American Psychological Association has set up a task force on the subject which regularly publishes a newsletter and which recently carried out a survey of professional openings for environmental psychologists.

In short, environmental psychology now exists. However, it is perhaps necessary, before embarking on a review of the research in this field, to ask why it started and why there is the present interest in the environment? Why has the quality of life, accepted uncritically for generations, become the subject of polemic? The first explanation which comes to mind is linked to technical progress. The industrialization which this has brought about, together with the growth in the population, has clearly been beneficial, but it has also had unforeseen negative consequences. The growth of knowledge and the multiplicity of more and more sophisticated, but increasingly cheap, consumer goods are factors in progress which provide evidence for the role of human ingenuity in improving living conditions. In reality, however, modern industry has often created working conditions which lead to alienation and decreased satisfaction when compared with traditional craft activities. In addition, industrialization often leads to use of the worst possible sites for urban concentrations. Is the abundance of cheap products sufficient justification for the poor working and social conditions of industrial workers? Need we put up with the brutalizing production line just because this lowers the price of cars so that the workers themselves can afford them? Even this equation is deceptive. Technical progress does not automatically improve the quality of life. The motor car is a particularly good example. The owner of an automobile certainly has more freedom and comfort than someone without one, and the driver at the wheel does experience a real feeling of power. But this is only true when there are few vehicles. Driving on uncrowded roads does give independence and a broader horizon. On the other hand, to suffer traffic jams and parking problems is to experience slavery and alienation. What should really be an improvement in our relationship with the environment becomes a source of pollution, disfiguring beauty spots, and an increase in the number of fatal accidents.

More generally, the advantages of urbanization do not always compensate for the disadvantages of poor, rapidly developed cities. Grouping industries close to the sources of primary materials and transport routes has created unplanned growth. Dormitory towns have become large, anonymous agglomerations which provide a minimum of comfort and a seedbed for vandalism and criminality because of their frustrating community life. Their inhabitants lose contact with nature, become the victims of dull uniformity, and are subject to inhuman modes of living in which they are deprived of the social support mechanisms found in rural communities and even in the old slums. Tourism is a similar paradox. People from cities seek nature by gathering together in huge numbers, damaging the most attractive places so that they rapidly lose the qualities of quietness and authenticity which people come for.

The exploitation of natural resources, the careless use of agrochemicals, and the construction of road networks, airports, and railway lines destroy the ecological balance and the quality of landscapes, as well as endangering health. This environmental upheaval has not taken into account the desirability of a balance between technological achievement and psychological and social needs. It is clear that physiological equilibrium and human sensitivity now stand threatened. The environment which we are creating for ourselves is no longer satisfactory.

The problems of environmental planning cannot be solved by going into reverse, even if there were individuals or communities who could reject technical progress and find places where the traditional ways of life have been preserved. On the other hand, it is not necessary to behave as if all of the criticisms made above of industrial cities and tourist spots apply to all situations. It is demonstrably true that a highway, a holiday village, or a factory can be beautiful, can merge into the landscape, and can meet the needs of the people for whom it was built. We need, however, to increase the research activity which will define the rules to be followed in order to ensure that a planned environment preserves its essential characteristics and satisfies those who live and work in it. In these decisions, a major role has been played first by economic factors and then by biological ones. It is only recently that the environmental experts and psychologists have suddenly realized the importance of the environment in mental life and the necessity of taking into account psychological factors in managing and protecting the environment. This sudden awareness had two facets: one of principle and the other of social values.

In principle, it has been known for a long time that the environment has an influence on human behavior. Since Lewin presented the formula, $B = f(P, E)$, it has been clearly recognized that behaviors (B) are a function of personal factors (P), as well as of the environment (E) in which they take place. However, psychological research has developed an imbalance, depending upon whether field work or laboratory techniques have been used. In the former, there has been more emphasis on showing relationships between the individual's psychological traits and his behavior than between the environment and behavior. In the latter, environment/behavior relations have been investigated, but at the micro- rather than macro-level, thus having little relevance to real life.

It needed the present environmental crisis to make people realize how badly understood have been the effects of the environment on individual behavior and, in the long term, on the personal characteristics of the individual. Some fields of applied psychology have already led the way. Thus, occupational psychologists have shown both that it is possible to treat the environment scientifically in research, and that this is worth doing. They have demonstrated that physical conditions have an important influence on the rate and quality of work. They have also investigated the broader field in which the environment is taken as all the structural and social characteristics of an organization. Many studies have made clear how organizational variables such as size, number of levels in the hierarchy, distribution of authority, social climate, control systems, information flow, and so forth are variables which modulate the relationships between individual characteristics and behavior. At present, environmental psychology does not possess models which are as well articulated as those available to organizational psychologists, but the quantity of research in the environmental field is increasing. There is work, for example, on the relationships between the school environment and educational progress, and how the stresses of pollution (particularly noise, lack of space, and freedom of action) impair free psychological functioning or necessitate adaptive behaviors which disrupt personal equilibrium.

It is not the importance of values and hierarchies of needs which has attracted attention to the dynamic processes of environmental choice, but the *variety* of needs, opinions, and preferences. This variability has not yet been adequately analyzed. However, its existence is not in doubt and its consequence is also well-known: The wishes and perceived alternatives of the decision-makers (planners, architects, and the like) cannot be generalized to the whole population. The relationship between each individual and his environment, his requirements from the environment, and his adaptive capabilities are all a function of personal characteristics both psychological and sociological, as well as of his own experience. Kurt Lewin was also a pioneer in proposing that the *valence* of an object can only be defined with reference to each individual's environmental *field*. To put it another way, the wishes of each individual in regard to the environment are related to the psychological traits and the personal history of that individual.

In short, environmental psychology not only exists, but meets a contemporary need. It has therefore developed rapidly with only a loose structure because of its atheoretical origins. The extensive but disparate variety of studies, together with the absence of an overall theoretical scheme, has been criticized frequently by Proshansky. This, without doubt, relates to the fact that psychologists have attempted to resolve nearly all the concrete problems put to them, without having the time to think about fundamental methodology, to construct general models, or even to evaluate different investigative techniques. The application of psychology to the problem of the environment seemed to be no more than using laboratory results to investigate more complex environments than those found in real life.

Put another way, it is possible that no one took the trouble, initially, to construct a theoretical framework, because one could be borrowed from existing general psychology. There are precedents for such a situation, particularly in the investigation of contemporary problems such as racial prejudice, social conflict, and the influence of the mass media, where studies have used the theories, concepts, and methods of experimental social psychology. This approach, however, does not seem open to environmental psychology, because it is extremely dissimilar to laboratory psychology, with the meaning of key concepts such as stimulus and environment differing greatly in the two contexts.

The experimenter uses the word stimulus when he relates the physical properties of the outside world (as expert observation reveals them) to the facts of perception. He therefore concerns himself with visual illusions, sensory limits, and with the manner in which perception is structured and acquires meaning. In short, he constructs the psychology of a living person by comparing the "objective" world with the "experienced" one. But the stimuli which he detaches from reality in order to increase his knowledge are artificial. They have to be fixed, stable, and uncontaminated: nonsense syllables, geometric shapes, and sounds rather than noises. Because of this, the continuous cycle of interrelations between, on the one hand, an environment which is multidimensional and changing, and, on the other, a person who continually adapts to his environment because it is where he must live, cannot be observed. The person studied in the laboratory is only a passive observer who receives information from the external world. The behavior observed is that of someone who deals with the flow of information in an environment over which he has no control. The "stimulus" of the laboratory bears no relation to environmental information received in the real world.

When the general psychologist puts the subject back into his own surroundings, he is interested in the negative and positive effects of those surroundings on that individual. Environmental research can be concerned with the influence of the physical environment on human behavior, for instance, laboratory studies of qualitative and quantitative changes in performance as a function of noise, temperature, or illumination. More often, the term environment is used in the restricted sense of social environment, in which case research looks for the effects of cultural handicap, family climate, or educational context upon the development of the individual, upon his personality, and upon his behavior. But whether or not we consider the laboratory stimulus or the environment *in situ,* that environment is studied as something to which the individual is passively subject, either because the individual is presented with unalterable conditions, or because social conservatism and the poverty of cultural environment are studied as burdens upon the person which limit his freedom of action and his personal progress.

It would be ridiculous to claim that there could be a psychology which did not take account of the environment. Nonetheless, the concept of environment found in general psychology has nothing to do with that upon which environmental psychology is based. Certainly, the results of experiments have been widely used by the new environmental specialists, particularly where the relationship between the perception of external surroundings and behavior within those surroundings is concerned. Architects have known how to use the laws of perception to create particular visual effects for a very long time (the proportions of Greek temples take into account the perception of perspective). The investigations which are now grouped under the heading of environmental psychology, however, go much further, and by different routes. They present five new features which map out a specific territory within psychology and which together form a unity.

The first and most fundamental point is that environmental psychology studies the relationship between man and environment dynamically. Man is adapting continuously and actively to his surroundings by changing both himself and the environment. What interests the environmental psychologist to the greatest degree are the ways in which these active exchanges occur and the complex algorithm of successive decision points. Craik (1970) has shown (in a chapter in *New Directions in Psychology*) that the environmental psychologist poses three basic questions. The first two are classic questions for psychology: What effect does the ordinary physical environment have upon people? and How do people understand their physical environment? The third question, however, is new and throws a new light upon the first two, to the extent that answers to them can also elucidate the answer to: What do people do to their physical environment?

Second, environmental psychology is concerned, above all, with the physical environment; either the natural environment untouched by the hand of man, or the built environment, particularly that of the city, as is clear from reading Craik's three questions. Social aspects do not enter into the environmental studies in any primary sense. But in reality, the social dimension is always there, because it constitutes the web of the relationships between man and environment. The environment is the framework of life, and life is never organized in isolation. Proshansky has encapsulated this: "The physical environment which we build is as much social as physical. The built world, whether we are talking about a school, a hospital, a house or a highway, is simply the specific expression of a social system which has a general influence upon our activities and our relations with others" (Proshansky, 1976). The physical environment simultaneously symbolizes, makes concrete, and conditions the social environment.

Third, the environment must be studied at the molar level rather than at the molecular or analytic. This means that people's reactions to their environment and their behavior within it can be investigated realistically only if the environment is a whole, and not made up of atomistic segments simply because the researcher is interested in an individual aspect of the environment. For example, the effects of noise on man cannot be considered independently of other situational characteristics (space, light, the meaning of the noise, previous experience of noise, and so forth) under the pretext that the only interest is in the effects of noise. The same point can be made for architectural space, temperature, or signposting. There are no simple relationships between an individual and isolated aspects of his environment.

In the fourth place, variation in behavior is not totally explained by the physical characteristics of the environment. Put more simply, the behavior of the individual in his environment is not only a set of responses to the real world and its range of physical variations. The environment is not a field of possible stimuli, but a collection of objectives, good and bad. As Lewin has shown, the behavior of man in his life-space cannot be understood without reference to the field of forces which represent the set of values attached to each aspect of the environment. Therefore, environmental psychology is inseparable from an analysis of motivation which is complete enough to allow us to understand why such an object is desired or not, and from an inventory of basic needs which man wishes to satisfy by means of and within his environment.

Finally, environmental psychology is above all an applied science, since it came into existence because of actual problems. It therefore has to be multidisciplinary in word and deed. The relatively ill-structured quality of present-day knowledge in this field can be put down to this practical orientation, as well as to its rapid development and interdisciplinary nature. In some areas, the problem of methodological validity arises, although some research, possibly questionable in this respect, has already found applications. Within some fields there are large gaps, while for others, there are many, often contradictory, findings. That is why this little book seeks only to arouse the interest of the reader and to inform him, without any claim to being exhaustive. The first chapter reviews theories, concepts, and methodological thinking. The four subsequent chapters look at current knowledge in light of Craik's three questions, which seem to cover the basic dimensions of research and activity in environmental psychology: How does man perceive and evaluate the built and natural environments in which he lives? How do the characteristics of the environment (and in particular the stresses) affect human behavior? How is space used for social purposes? What is man's active role in planning the environment, either in conserving nature or in actively designing it? In concluding the book, a tentative sketch of the future development of this new discipline is presented on the basis of a balance drawn between the obstacles encountered and the scientific progress made.

CHAPTER 1

Models, Concepts, and Methods

Environmental psychology developed rapidly under the pressure of events, and if psychologists have taken risks in this new discipline, it has been in an attempt to respond to the problems posed by architects, planners, economists, and/or legislators. Research attended to practical questions, for example, the establishment of the levels of noise exposure at which psychological well-being is endangered. How can the design of those parts of buildings which are shared encourage social interaction? How should classrooms be laid out to encourage the development of young children? Is the progress of a mental patient aided by specific arrangements of hospital services? What is the influence of office size, or the number of occupants in a room, upon work performance?

No general principles are available for answering these questions rationally, and therefore, when asked to tackle them, psychologists carried out pieces of applied research, quite naturally trying to use classic experimental designs and conventional measurement instruments. However, the unsuitability of theoretical approaches borrowed from laboratory psychology soon became apparent: the multiplicity of independent variables and the interactions between them, the necessity to take into account simultaneously the social, cultural, and physical environments, and the large interindividual and intergroup differences all combine to make clear analysis and generalization from the results very perilous. The traditional instruments also proved to be inadequate. Thus, every one of the psychologists concerned did his best from the very start to invent methods and then, after the event, to systematize (at least partially) these new ideas and methodologies. None of this was without difficulties, many of which still have not been surmounted. At present, the majority of environmental psychologists would agree that a new theoretical and conceptual framework is required, and everyone would agree that this has not yet been satisfactorily created. We will begin, therefore, with a discussion of the problems which confront the environmental psychologist in his attempt to build a coherent theoretical scheme. We will then describe the existing approaches and the methodologies in use.

The absence of a corpus of theory and the uncertainty about methodology have become a permanent concern of a growing number of psychologists who are active in this field. One can see evidence of this in, for example, the chapter about methodological problems which Proshansky and his colleagues (1976) place at the head of the most recent edition of their book of readings, in which Proshansky, Moos, Ittelson, and Altman each deal with the possibility of building a theoretical framework and describe the difficulties encountered by environmental psychology in elaborating a new methodology suited to field research intended to aid decision-making and action. They explain these difficulties, just as we have, by reference to the youth of the discipline and its mission, and to its orientation toward the immediate solution of practical problems. These are, however, only short-term difficulties for the discipline. Organizational psychology, occupational psychology, and counselling, to give only a few examples, originally suffered the same constraints and have nonetheless produced fruitful theoretical models.

Other explanations are possible for the theoretical lacunae which now exist in this field. Ittelson reminds us that traditional psychology offers a perspective on man's actions upon the exterior environment (his creativity and innovation) which is totally different from the way it looks at the effects of the environment on man.

As Ittelson argues (in Proshansky et al., 1976):

The man/environment dichotomy has led to a notion of a dichoto-
mous man, man the responder to environments on the one hand,
and man the creator of environments on the other, both of whom
stand separate from an external environment which itself is split
into those aspects which are sources of responses and those which
are products of human activities.

Environmental psychology's problem, according to Ittelson, is
precisely that of uniting these two domains, not only by building
a bridge between them, but by creating a complete model in
which the two aspects are as integrated as they are in real life.

It is possible to analyze this dichotomy further. The man
creating the environment and the man who is subject to it belong, implicitly, to different social categories. On the one hand,
the decision-maker, who has the responsibility; on the other, the
plain citizen who puts up with an environment thought up by
others. Taylor et al. (1965) distinguished two professional roles:
the manager, who plans and organizes work, and the worker,
who carries it out without thought or initiative. This segregation of function has caused a great deal of hostility and has
never corresponded with reality, either in business or anywhere
else. In fact, environmental action takes place at many different
levels, from the design of a block of apartments, an office, a
factory, or even a neighborhood by architects and planners, to
arranging your own room to suit your personal preferences.

In the second place, creative people are seen by the psychologist from the viewpoint of individual differences: individuals
are differentially capable (because of their skills, their intellect,
or their personality) of conceiving and creating an environment. The study of "the person who creates environments" will
be based on individual typology and on the analysis of factors
which are favorable to the aptitude or the desire to create something. On the other hand, the people who respond to the environment are seen as homogeneous; the scientific aim is then to
discern general laws which apply to all individuals and to predict the psychological effects of a given environment, for all
people and whatever effects. The traditional desire for rigorous
experimental design (with an independent variable, a dependent variable, and generalizable results) is apparent here. Un-

fortunately, in the real world no variable can be controlled totally, and any model of the interactions between variables must
either remain vague and abstract or take this complexity into
account. There is no ideal environment, nor a mode of living
with invariant effects: the general culture and individual experiences play important and very diverse roles as moderating
variables.

Environmental psychology must therefore integrate these
compartmentalized concepts of man, removing the barriers between each of the specified fields of psychological concern: man
as he differs from others, perceiving man, social man, learning
man. This necessity imposes a series of constraints which cause
difficulties in the creation of theoretical schemes. Proshansky
(1976) recently put forward a list which is relevant to these
constraints. His first point is that the environmental psychologist must study only the real world, outside the laboratory, so as
to preserve "the absolute integrity of person/physical setting
events." Let us take a simple example of the methodological
difficulties which this implies. Those investigations of noise
annoyance which are carried out in the laboratory with recorded noises do not give results which are directly generalizable to real life. Why not? Because essentially, annoyance is
strongly influenced by each individual's affective and social
evaluation of the noise heard. Noise has a meaning in real life
which goes beyond its mere physical presence. The environment
which we study in real life is simultaneously a collection of
physical data and psychological data that are deeply inter-
twined, one with the other. Any theory of noise annoyance must
take into account a complex collection of nonadditive factors
which do not lend themselves to easy analysis.

The second constraint is that environmental psychology is
always concerned with two different orders of phenomena: the
behavioral and the verbal. Normally, it is the social psychologist who asks questions and deals with attitudes and opinions,
and the experimentalist who observes behavior. In our case,
however, the researcher is forced to deal simultaneously with
verbal information about the experiences of individuals in different environments and with the observation of their

behavior—and to reconcile the often contradictory results of these two approaches. It is quite possible that the subjective adaptation to the environment (and particularly to nuisance) which is essential if the individual is to survive and be comfortable is achieved only at some psychological cost, and therefore at a genuine social cost. In other words, the fact that an environment is perceived as adequate by those who live in it does not mean that they do not suffer harmful effects in the long or the short run. Incidentally, this creates a major difficulty for the psychologist in communicating his results to planners, for two reasons. The first is that most decision-makers tend to accept survey results which agree with their own intuitions. The second is that the apparent satisfaction of individuals often seems to them to be a sufficient criterion for the quality of life. We therefore still need to find out what is necessary for efficient environmental communication.

The third problem is defined by Proshansky as the orientation of environmental psychology towards meaning. By meaning, Proshansky understands

> the meaning and nature of these events as they are defined by geographical locations, designed purposes, intended and actual activities, and the character of the actors involved.

In other words, behind the same behavior, or the same attitude, there are motivations, hierarchies or values, and structures of needs which can be extremely different. It is the meaning of behavior, or better still, the scenes and settings of behavior, which we must learn to understand and analyze. From the point of view of the creation of explanatory models, this clearly complicates the whole affair.

The fourth point concerns the temporal dimension. No analysis of man/environment relations can be complete if it excludes the past and the future. The past, because the experience of each individual is summated as the meaning of the environment; the future, because action on the environment and the uses made of it are functions of the plans made for the future and of individual expectations. Furthermore, the environment itself has a past and represents a form of collective memory. A taste for old things cannot be explained only by their artistic value. The need for roots and historical links in a country or a region shows the importance of temporal dimensions in relations between people, objects, and geographical realities.

Proshansky's concluding remarks constitute a synthesis of all the above observations: there is no physical environment which is not at the same time a social and cultural environment. Not only does every alteration in the environment possess a cultural significance and entail social consequences, but it is especially true that every behavior is a response to both a physical environment and a social one. Taken as a whole, this examination shows the necessity of combining the separate perspectives of social and individual psychology. This is clearly an ambitious project which cannot be realized by the direct application of existing theoretical models. In fact, the first theoretical approach of environmental psychologists was to look for formulations of their basic postulate (the necessity to study the environment holistically) in the classics of psychological literature.

THEORETICAL THEMES

Three early theorists can be invoked: Tolman, Brunswik, and Lewin. As a reaction to the S-R (stimulus-response) scheme, which describes the environment exclusively in terms of impersonal stimuli and universally shared goals, Tolman (1932) recommended a global or "holistic" approach, taking into account those intervening variables which are responsible for perception. This implied that individuals' responses to the environment cannot be explained without the complete analysis of intermediate cognitive stages, since it is these stages which confer a personal meaning on the stimuli received from the environment. Brunswik (1956) puts the same sort of emphasis on perceptual processes and underlines the importance of perceptual representation in relation to each person. According to Brunswik, all the information coming from the environment has a specific validity for each subject. This explains the variety of cognitive representations which can be seen when two subjects are placed in the same environment; the weight given to each piece of information, its likelihood, and the manner in which coordination is achieved make personal interpretations of the external world unique to the individual.

Although Lewin did not pay any particular attention to the physical world, he was the first psychologist to propose a coherent theoretical structure corresponding to the needs of environmental psychology. It is true that some of his theoretical postulates are based on abstract propositions which are very attractive but not tested, and perhaps testable only with difficulty. It is equally true that the research of his pupils and disciples uses relatively few of the concepts and theoretical models which he proposed. The influence of Lewin and his contribution to environmental psychology exists at a different level, that of the general orientation of psychology and its relation to action in the real world—more specifically, of three points which concern the role of the psychologist, and the aims and methods of his research. In his youth a philosopher of science in Germany, Lewin later became a psychologist preoccupied with the application of the discipline. He frequently stressed (1946, 1948) that the scientist must have a social conscience and concern himself with improving the world and the society in which he lives. This is, of course, one of the explicit motivations of the environmental psychologist, who has the objective of *optimizing* the environment to suit the aspirations of those living in it. Although Lewin was influenced by the Gestalt school, he was not limited to the study of processes of perception. Quite the contrary, he included in his theoretical scheme individual needs and values, as well as the individual's cognitive and affective characteristics, since they give to each object present in the life-space a positive or negative valence. In doing this, he shows clearly that central psychological processes (cognition, motivation, goal-directed behavior) must be the principal topics of research, rather than peripheral sensory and motor processes. At the same time, he emphasizes the interdependence of psychological events, which cannot be analyzed in isolation or explained without taking their interrelations into account.

More concretely, Lewin's definition of the "force field" can be considered an inventory of tendencies capable of determining behavior in the environment. There are not only the characteristics of the perceiver (individual or group), but also the region which the force field mobilizes inside the life-space, the force represented by the changes that the field can induce and the nature of those changes; the quality of the origin of the forces (friendly or hostile, personal or neutral) and the attributes of the source which give it its power. This list is directly relevant as a guide for an environmental research project. We could apply it to the experimental investigation of the effect of aircraft noise on the behavior of a group of people living near an airport. Their behavior can be determined by the characteristics of the noise, the nature of the activities disturbed by the noise, the importance of those activities, what can be done to protect them from the noise, the attitudes of the group towards the airport, the relations of the airport to social and community life, and the circumstances which led to the airport's location. It is obvious that the behavior of the group is not determined directly by simple sensory processes. At the methodological level, Lewin is the pioneer of action research, which consists in essence of studying changes as they occur in the real-world context of the dynamic processes involved—in situ study that excludes neither experimental method nor rigorous observation. In sum, it is not surprising that all major reviews of environmental psychology cite Lewin and make him the point of departure and reference for their work.

Obviously, with Tolman as with Lewin, it is not a matter solely of general position and concepts. Deeper analyses and models which are closer to concrete problems are also necessary. Moves have been made in this direction already. In 1954, in an article which passed relatively unremarked because psychologists were not at that time sensitized to environmental problems, Chein discussed the basis of the theoretical schemes of Tolman and Lewin—the distinction drawn by Kofka (1935) between a geographical environment (physical and social) and a behavioral environment (the environment perceived by an individual and to which he responds). Chein considered this dichotomy to be unjustified and proposed a synthetic concept, the geobehavioral environment, consisting of everything in the geographical environment which can be used to explain behavior.

He describes distinct categories of objects in this environment: stimuli (the possible agents of change in the stream of activity); goal objects (which can serve as need satisfiers); noxiants (which can produce unpleasantness or pain); supports or constraints (which make particular behaviors feasible or preclude them); directors (which give direction to behavior); and physical and social currents (which provide a normative framework and help to differentiate roles).

ENVIRONMENTAL MODELS

These differing theories (of Tolman, Lewin, and Chein) preceded the development of environmental psychology as an independent discipline. They provided a base to be used for applied research into man/environment relations, but such efforts must be made specific. This has already happened to a limited extent as researchers have attempted to synthesize the results of specialized research projects, or as theoreticians (however few in number) have attempted to justify their own approach to the methodology or problems of environmental psychology by supporting it with a more general conception of the relations between man and his environment. If one attempts to classify these theoretical attempts so as to deal with them in a systematic fashion, it becomes clear that they fall into two categories according to whether they hold to an essentially determinist view of the relation between man and his environment or whether they analyze the processes of interaction between man and his environment and investigate how individual personality structures the way in which the environment is perceived and understood. They are not, in any case, opposed theoretical conceptions; in reality, they concern two perspectives on environmental psychology. At the present time, there is no unified theory which covers the perception of the environment, action about the environment, and the influence of the environment upon the individual.

As far as the first group of approaches is concerned, Festinger was a pioneer. In the 1950s, in collaboration with Schachter and Back, he carried out a study of the determinants of friendship

networks and of the influence of the network on the formation of
attitudes and opinions. This study was carried out among students living in a veterans' residence at the Massachusetts Institute of Technology. This group was extremely homogeneous
with regard to age, marital status, social class origins, and
present interests. Analysis of the interviews with the wives
showed that the proximity of dwellings determined the number
of contacts between residents; these contacts, not chosen by the
subjects themselves, were nonetheless the basis of friendship
links; friendship networks and social relations determined information flows and attitudes and opinions. Within the groups
of buildings which formed a closed courtyard, attitudes and collective behavior were very homogeneous; the greatest number
of nontypical residents were found to be living in the buildings
which were on the edges of the residence and thus outwardly
oriented. In short, social life, opinions, and participation in
group activities were greatly influenced by the proximity of
buildings to one another. It is only a small step from this to
talking about "architectural determinism," a step too easily
taken for the taste of Broady (1966), who poses the question of
whether architecture exerts a direct and clear influence upon
people's behavior. Does the environment condition us? Broady
criticizes this method for oversimplifying the problems, and
accuses architects of using this argument to increase their importance and exaggerate their social role. Nonetheless, Terence
Lee (1968), the English psychologist, defends an analogous
thesis in his study of the neighborhood. But he adds a more
complete analysis of the cognitive processes by which the private environment comes into being, and his conclusions are to
some extent more on the activist side of the argument: behavior
is not passively determined by the environment; there are people who plan their environment according to objectives related
to social values, where physical factors and social dimensions
are very closely interlinked. He uses the concept of schema,
which was defined by its originator, Bartlett, as "an active organization of past reactions and experiences," to investigate the
neighborhood as a sociospatial, "man-environment" representation created by his research subjects and enabling them, on the

basis of personal experiences, to differentiate the neighborhood from the rest of the environment. The housewives interviewed were able to delimit their neighborhood on a local map, thus describing an "invisible landscape." When, on the basis of the interviews, an analysis of the content of these areas was performed, it could be seen that they included the friends most frequently visited, the shops at which purchases were made, and the locations of facilities used. In addition, Lee calculated a "neighborhood quotient": the number of houses, shops, and so forth in each subject's area expressed as a function of the total number in the locality. He was able to show that the number rose with increasing social class and length of residence, and that it was linked with the husband's place of work and place of birth. In short, every individual's experience determined his/her representation of the environment and his/her links with that environment.

It is clear that for Terence Lee, the psychological process mediating the relationship between the individual and the environment is essentially cognitive. Past experience and acquired links with the environment determine how it is represented. Since everyone's experience is individual, it follows that each representation is unique and in turn determines the individual's behavior in that environment. Other causal links have been proposed in explanation of architectural determinism. Wilner suggests that improving the quality of life increases the degree of affiliation with a social class and, because of this, makes the individual formulate higher social aspirations and adhere to a different set of social values. It is probable that the external environment reflects a better self-image as the quality of life increases, but this remains to be demonstrated. For the moment, one can do no more than point to the supporting studies in occupational psychology which investigate the self-concept as a mediating variable between motivation and success: success increases self-esteem and makes the individual set himself higher goals; it also motivates him towards achieving those goals. On the other hand, as Mercer (1975) has noted, it is equally well-known that poverty of environment retards the development of self-concept in young children. It is the variety of perceptual experience which in fact allows the child to differentiate itself from the exterior world.

Oscar Newman's thesis in his book, *Defensible Space* (1972), proposes another mediating variable which supports architectural determinism. He is particularly interested in petty crime and vandalism, and compares the characteristics of blocks of apartments where the frequency of such events is low with those where it is high. He interprets his results as showing that in large, multistory units, people lock themselves away in their own apartments and feel no concern for what happens outside. He thinks this is because the number and variety of residents in these large urban units make collective action in defense of the shared spaces impossible. According to Newman, therefore, the architect should construct an environment which arouses in residents the wish to defend it and to create a communal life involving every individual in everybody else's security. To do this, it is necessary to avoid an exaggeratedly "public" appearance for the spaces between dwellings and for common access areas and corridors, so that they do not look as if they do not belong to anyone. On the contrary, they must look like extensions of dwellings, restricted to specific residents who can and must watch over them. In addition, these shared spaces should be sufficiently attractive for people not to see them as barriers between themselves and their neighbors, or as symbolic of a poor environment. The idea that petty crime is provoked by an aggressive environment, apparently not belonging to anyone and not subject to any surveillance, is implicit in Newman's hypothesis, as is the unpremeditated nature of the undesired events. To put it another way, there are environments which encourage vandalism, rather than vandals who will always vandalize somewhere. Additionally, Newman emphasizes that we must keep a check on this aspect of architectural determinism. Thus, when the Pruitt-Igoe apartment blocks, built in 1954 to replace slums in St. Louis, became the site of acts of vandalism and repeated violence to such an extent that people did not want to live in them anymore, the buildings were partially demolished in 1972. It is therefore clear that the built environment facilitates or discourages some behaviors. If society disapproves of these behaviors, it modifies or destroys the environment. After the events of 1968, the streets of the Boulevard St. Michel in Paris were replaced by tarmac (unsuitable for the construction of barricades), and the lecture halls of the Sorbonne were progressively reorganized so as to accommodate offices and administrative services.

In the works of Festinger, Lee, and Newman, architectural determinism is used as a concept linking the environment and a range of specific behaviors: social life, vandalism, and community activities. A much more general model has been proposed by Roger Barker (1968), a pupil and disciple of Lewin who, under the title of "ecological psychology," has proposed a theory which utilizes new concepts and justifies the methodology which Barker and his followers applied to the development of his initial model. Instead of the separate study of on the one hand, people, and on the other, the environment (and the influence of the one on the other), Barker recommended the study of the sites in which behaviors take place (behavior-settings). These settings have exact spatial boundaries, definite times for behavior, and possess a structure in which physical and social elements are closely associated with the cultural context of the setting. All of these elements together have a strong influence upon the range of behaviors which can be exhibited in a given setting. For example, a church is a behavior-setting just as much as a classroom, a pharmacy, or a football ground, but the behaviors exhibited in each of these cannot be interchanged. This theory has three important consequences: (1) the environment, seen in this way, is dependent upon its inhabitants, who use regulatory behavior (plans, timetabling, organized activities) to preserve the characteristics of the settings. The physical environment has a goal, desired and maintained by the community, which determines the behaviors exhibited there and prevents those which should not occur. (2) However, the environment-behavior relationship is not rigid: there are individual differences, since the behavior-setting is particular to each individual because of his own behavioral characteristics. Thus the same highway (the example comes from Barker) is different for the fast, as compared with the slow, driver. Everything con-

spires to speed up the slow driver, but all the information which
the fast driver receives (the behavior of traffic police, the difficulty of negotiating bends in the road and of passing other vehicles) tends to slow him down. (3) There is not only interindividual variability within the same setting, but also ecological
variability in the settings themselves. In particular, the behavior-setting can be under- or overmanned. Barker and his colleagues, studying schools and religious communities, have
shown that the less populated a setting, the more numerous and
varied the behaviors of each person. The opposite is equally
true: participation decreases as the population increases. There
exists, therefore, an ecological determinism in which the causal
variables are neither exclusively psychological nor exclusively
environmental, but are linked to the man/environment systems
as wholes.

Barker's theoretical framework has important methodological implications. It implies that the psychology of the environment must be limited to natural behavior—which he calls T-
data (T for transducer)—unbiased by the experimenter, who
confines himself to noting, classifying and interpreting spontaneous behaviors which would occur were he not there. In contrast, he proscribes the use of O-data, observed in subjects
placed in artificial environments. In fact, the environment
which produces the effects it is desired to study is not a neutral
variable but a datum closely linked to its inhabitants and pos-
sessing a meaning which they have elaborated and which they
control.

In short, the idea that the environment has an influence on
behavior, which corresponds with common sense, is proposed
and exemplified by a variety of authors who, as a group, refuse
to translate the idea into a mechanical determinism. The environment acts by means of the ways in which it is represented,
which gives it a highly subjective character because of the very
different experiences of each individual. In addition, the individual does not submit passively to the environment. He con-
trols it in line with his goals. Because of this, the environment
represents a tool which can be modified, abandoned, or de-
stroyed if social or other goals are abandoned or not achieved.
Even if laboratory experiments show that a particular aspect of

the physical environment determines a particular molecular behavior, the two kinds of variables (environmental and psychological) have been removed from their context and therefore do not correspond to reality, since they are both too simple and too complex. Proximity had a strong influence upon the social network of the inhabitants of Westgate, but it is only one factor in a complex chain. Had the characteristics of their social life failed to correspond to their social values and needs, they might well have abandoned the buildings, as did those inhabitants of St. Louis who lived in Pruitt-Igoe, and perhaps as city-dwellers who do move away from urban centers. The "negotiated" nature of this environmental determinism is much clearer in Barker. The concept of the behavior-setting has no meaning except in a transactional perspective. Clearly, a church does determine the behaviors which take place there, but this is because men built it with clear designs and the social group would react coercively if there were inappropriate behaviors. The environment determines behavior because individuals who are present and vigilant make it do so. It is noteworthy that both meaning and determinism have disappeared from historic sites which are no longer used, like the great Aztec temples of Mexico.

Moreover, there is no essential opposition between the determinist theories just reviewed and the "interactive" models which, essentially, attempt to elaborate new concepts so as to bypass the traditional man/environment dichotomy. What these authors wanted to examine was the role of personality in man-environment interactions. In the same way as none of the preceding theories had proposed that it was possible to predict behaviors directly from the characteristics of the environment, so none of them had put forward the narrow view in which personality traits are the sole determinants of behavior. It is preferable to talk about specific individual needs and environmental conditions which allow (or prevent) their satisfaction or of personality factors which introduce personal biases into the perception of the environment. Mischel (1973) emphasizes that the diversity of human behavior in different situations cannot be predicted in terms of personality factors. The correlations observed between these and actual behavior are usually low and, Mischel adds, no correspondence can be demonstrated between the answers given to questionnaires and actual behavior. To explain behavior in the environment, it is necessary to take account of the functional properties of that environment. With this in view, Mischel proposes the idea of "behaviour-contingency units," which are concrete representations of the behavior-environment relationship as seen by the individual. He emphasizes the social learning which establishes the links between specific environmental conditions and appropriate modes of response.

The continual interaction between individual needs, environmental perception, and the satisfaction of individual goals is just as central in Kaplan's (1972, 1977) model. In his view, each cognitive representation of the environment is determined (and possibly distorted) by four fundamental needs common to everybody: to recognize, predict, evaluate, and act. As Charles Mercer has noted (1975), this implies an orientation towards the future, because these needs must also be satisfied in the future, and decisions made by the individual must foresee future needs. Peter Jay (1968; also cited by Mercer) proposes the addition of the past as well in taking expectations into account, since each individual "compares what he has with what he has a reasonable right to expect, and is satisfied if the comparison is favourable and otherwise complains" (Mercer, 1975: 54). This necessity to take into account past requirements, which are either recent and hence conscious or stored in long-term memory and operating at the unconscious level, leads Marisa Zavalloni (1977) to propose a method of analyzing "representational units" which allows us to discern the "constructive properties of the mind" belonging to each individual, characteristic of his experience and conditioning his "representational conceptualization" which is responsible for "operant behavior" in the environment. It is possible to go further in that direction, like Sonnenfeld (1969), and look for an *environmental personality*—made up of all those traits which produce individual reactions to a common environment. Eysenck (1967) moves in the same direction when he puts forward the idea that extroverts need a greater variety of external stimulation than introverts.

The best organized theoretical scheme in this area is probably that presented by Kenneth Craik (1976) in his article, "The

Personality Research Paradigm in Environmental Psychology."
He suggests that to the two traditional questions of personality
research (How a person behaves in relation to himself and how a
person behaves in relation to others) must be added a third (How
a person behaves in relation to the physical environment). This
research orientation could be applied to the definition of a typology of environmental personalities, to the description of empirical environmental personalities in particular groups (for example, architects, hunters, and so on), and finally to the prediction
of behavior in specific situations. Craik's third question relates
to very concrete problems such as the decision to migrate and
the adaptation of the migrant to a new environment, the evaluation of the environment, behavior in natural catastrophes, or
even the selection of a dwelling or a neighborhood in which to
live.

From the theoretical point of view, Craik places himself
within the framework of the interaction between the person and
the environment. He refers specifically to such research as that
of Moos (1969) and Mehrabian and Russell (1974). Moos observed in a detailed manner the behavior of sixteen psychiatric
patients in six different environmental situations (interview,
individual therapy, group therapy, community meeting, lunch,
and free time). Analysis of variance of the behavior in terms of
individuals, situations, and individuals × situations shows that
there are behaviors linked with situations (talking, nodding
assent), others linked with individuals (smoking, smiling), but
that in most cases behavior is linked to the totality of the indi-
vidual/situation, particularly the different types of movements
or specific behaviors like wringing hands, scratching, picking
up objects, and the like. With the same intention, but with a
more artificial experimental scheme based on the analysis of
accounts given by subjects rather than by observing behavior,
Mehrabian and Russell showed that the pleasure expected by
different subjects from specific circumstances is strongly influenced by the relation between their personality and the characteristics of the situation.

These attempts at modelling the man-environment interaction are clearly still at the level of general principles. Nonetheless, it is striking that these authors have important common

points which relate just as closely to the methodological orientations of Cronbach (1975) and of Proshansky (1976, ch. 5). All of
them reject as artificial the investigation of or search for simple
relations between individual traits or behaviors and physical or
environmental characteristics. In Cronbach's view, this quest
for fundamental laws stems from the concern of psychologists to
belong to the natural sciences—despite the fact that almost all
psychological phenomena are the result of multiple, complexly
interacting variables. Thus, the authors whose theoretical positions have been described above are made to define the variables which permit the description of the structures of environmental representation, or of the environmental personality, or
even of behavior, thereby emphasizing the discovery of interactions and not the analysis of elements which lose their meaning
when taken in isolation. In addition, they all, like Proshansky,
stress the difference between "systems of behavioral reactions"
and "systems of psychological reactions." The former include
experiences of which the subject is unconscious. At one extreme,
they result from attitudes which have unconsciously crystal-
lized into a system of coherent and explicable opinions. The last
point emphasized by Proshansky and made equally obvious by
the other authors is that even if they focus their interest on the
representation of the environment as the mediator between environment and behavior, this representation is not uniquely
cognitive and in the present, but rather is conceived as the
result of the present and numerous past experiences. It takes
into account not only information from the physical world, but
also social and cultural data.

Perhaps a unitary theoretical model of man-environment relations is not possible. In fact, the point about which there is
total agreement is that in deciding to study such relations as a
whole, the great diversity and complexity of causal variables
are totally inescapable. A unique model would have to unite the
past and the future, perceptual processes and normative processes, behavioral and verbal data concerning the physical, psy-
chophysiological, and psychological problems of the individual,
as well as relations with the social and cultural environment,
and so on.

METHODS

The multiplicity of possible causal variables becomes still clearer when an attempt is made to assess the methods used in environmental psychology. The full range of possibilities has been used, from laboratory experiments following a rigorous factorial design (this has, of course, been criticized as an artificial reduction of reality) to spontaneous observations made without the knowledge of the subjects and without a previously established framework, via questionnaire techniques taken from social psychology of the most orthodox kind and projective techniques borrowed from clinical psychology. A purely descriptive approach to the methods which have been used would thus be of little interest. Therefore, we shall try to examine the methods according to the uses to which they have been put in environmental psychology: to explain and predict behaviors as a function of situations, as they actually exist. In order to do this, it would seem useful to start by introducing the three methodological options which are typical of any experimental work: the choice of *subjects;* the choice of an experimental *site;* and the choice of *techniques*. Clearly, the data follow from these three decisions, and the generalizability of the results is tightly defined by the options selected and their consequences.

The selection of *subjects* implicitly raises the problem of the relation between the results and the particular experimental sample. Specifically, the following question must be answered: Is what has been observed capable of verification with other groups of subjects? If not, which characteristics of the selected samples explain data gathered? Clearly this type of question opens the way for comparative research studies on different samples (it is to be regretted that this type of research is not common in environmental psychology). The beginnings of an answer to this may be found by carefully analyzing the common features of the subjects in a sample and by carrying out all the comparisons possible within the sample itself.

In reality, there is not always a free choice of subjects. Consequently, five approaches may be distinguished, three for field research and two for laboratory work.

(1) Research is carried out in the field and the sample includes all the subjects living (or working, or spending their leisure) at the chosen site. Rivlin and Wolfe (1972) systematically observed the behavior of all children resident in a new psychiatric hospital during the first, second, tenth, and thirty-first weeks after opening. In the same way, Chombart de Lauwe (1976) and her team investigated all the children living at selected sites in her studies of children.

(2) Having chosen the site, it is impossible to observe (or interview, or test) all the inhabitants. A sample is therefore drawn. Marans (1970) used this method in comparing four communities which had been developed in more or less planned ways. The sample was initially defined according to precise criteria—age and composition of the family, length of residence—and a random subsample of the families meeting these criteria was then chosen. The representativeness of this sample was then checked by standard social survey techniques.

(3) It is possible to choose an experimental sample selected from a larger group (not to be confused with 2 above) which does not, however, need to be representative. There are several possibilities. It could be that one subsample is more accessible than another, and that the interviews are therefore more often with housewives in apartment blocks (who work at home) than with their husbands (who work away). In theory, it is possible to adjust the sample. In practice, the problem will persist because there is a strong probability that the male population which has been observed or interviewed has specific characteristics (the sick, the out-of-work, nightworkers, and the like). The researcher might also decide to limit the sample for very specific reasons. John and Elizabeth Newson, for example, only interviewed mothers in their study of child development in Nottingham since, in their opinion, the mothers were likely to be better informed on the subject (1968). Likewise, the sample may be defined by the objectives of the study. Goledzinowski (1976) studied spatial perception in subway train travellers in Paris and limited his survey to people who specifically asked for spatial information, i.e., those who were lost. Self-selection of subjects at the site can also cause difficulties in the conduct of a survey. For instance, in a survey of the health of people living in the vicinity of Orly airport, the researchers observed that people who presented themselves voluntarily for a free medical examination were more often subject to severe medical conditions than the parent population at the selected site (J. Francois and J.G. Henrotte, personal communication).

(4) The fourth case is the one in which subjects, unselected, come to the laboratory so that their reactions to specific environments

can be investigated. Unfortunately, these volunteers are often psychology students, particularly in North America where participation in experiments is often an obligatory part of the curriculum. Examples of this are often found in studies of the social aspects of the environment, perhaps because the researchers are still influenced by experimental social psychology. For example, Freedman et al. (1971) studied the laboratory performance of subjects exposed to various degrees of crowding, Altman and Haythorn (1967) used naval volunteers in various studies of isolation, Canter (1974) used students to evaluate the decor of living rooms, and students took part as subjects in Stokols et al.'s (1973) study of the perception of crowding.

(5) The fifth case is quite rare and consists of choosing subjects for laboratory research who represent specific characteristics. Altman and Haythorn (1967) used this method to study territorial behavior in pairs of subjects who had lived in isolation for a number of days, but they matched subjects according to personality to produce "compatible" or "incompatible" pairs, e.g., two subjects, both with a strong need for dominance. In a current piece of research, Widlocher (personal communication) is examining the behavior, on several experimental tasks, of subjects chosen because they have a high level of exposure to noise at work.

The choice of the experimental *site* is particularly important in a branch of psychology for which the physical setting is not incidental to the research (i.e., it is only necessary to consider to the extent to which it *might* influence the results), but the major variable. It poses essentially the same type of problem as the choice of subjects—that of generalizability. Would the results be the same elsewhere? In reality, this question assumes a distinction which is rarely made explicitly, that between the *macrosite* and the *microsite*. The microsite is the object of the investigation—the room, the building, the office, or the school, the psychological effects of which are to be studied. But the office belongs to an organization, the room to a complete building, the building to a district, and the school is only one part of the educational system. All the sites are part of a region, with specific climate, culture, and geography. The macrosite, therefore, is the total of the surroundings of the site which is the focus of the investigation. It can alter the observed relationships between the characteristics of the microsite and the behavior of its occupants. Without taking this too far, it is known, in organizational psychology, that the technological and economic environments alter the effects of the size and structure of production units upon worker behavior.

This distinction shows the limitation of laboratory research. The environment can, on the one hand, be cut up into sensory slices: Glass and Singer (1972) were able in this way to observe behavior in different noise conditions in a systematic way; Lecuyer (1976) could study spatial grouping and its effect on the interactions between group members. Alternatively, the environment can be simulated so as to be evaluated and interpreted by the subjects who come to the laboratory. The simulation can be photographs with significant features (advertising billboards, electric cables, traffic signs, and the like) added or subtracted by the experimenter. Canter et al. (1974) used photographs and drawings of room interiors which systematically varied the angle of the ceiling, the size of the windows, and the arrangement of the furniture. Much more sophisticated simulations have been constructed, notably at the Berkeley Environmental Simulation Laboratory where a complex optical system can realistically reproduce all the movements that can be made in a landscape represented by a three-dimensional model (McKechnie, 1977). The validity of such simulations, when comparisons are made between subjects exposed to real environments and those exposed to various simulations, is very high. All of the work that has involved this type of comparison is in agreement on this finding (see McKechnie and Canter). And, of course, simulations have the advantage of allowing controlled variation in experimental conditions.

In short, in the laboratory it is possible either to study the relationship between artificially separated aspects of the environment and behavior, or to predict what evaluation of an environment would be made in the real world. In both cases, however, the environments are deprived of their social, cultural, and temporal contexts. The absence of the macrosite in the laboratory study probably explains the latent opposition between those researchers who follow the classical experimental model and those who, like Barker, Proshansky, and Sommer, prefer to carry out field research that studies the environment in its total and authentic state. These are positions which do not have to be taken up—rather, it has to be recognized that the two types of research have their own specific limitations. The laboratory gives the opportunity for the detailed study and identification of psychological processes. In practice, however, interrelationships are complex and the addition of incomplete links, even where well demonstrated in the laboratory, does not allow us to construct an overall framework for man-environment phenomena. Therefore, real field research is absolutely essential, because it allows us to see the whole range of variables and their structure in action, and because it includes temporal and sociocultural parameters.

The selection of techniques is obviously just as important as the choice of subjects and sites. Techniques must be selected in the light of precise hypotheses about the phenomena studied. Each technique leads to the collection of specific data which must be analyzed in terms of the hypotheses which caused those methods to be chosen. It is clear that a study using randomly chosen methods, with curiosity as the only guide, could only give results which would be just as random. It would seem, therefore, to be useful to classify the methods used by environmental psychologists according to the information which they produce.

Table 1.1 shows the different methods used in relation to the data obtained directly by these methods. There has, for obvious reasons, been no attempt to deal with the interpretations which can be made of the data. Six categories of data are distinguished:

(1) actions made by the individual upon his environment; this could include both his arrangement of his private space and activity concerned with public spaces;

(2) perceived effects upon behavior, i.e., those effects which the individual describes as associated with his own experience of the environment;

(3) effects which the experimenter links to environmental variations but which the subject has not been prompted to link in that way;

(4) environmental cognition, i.e., the way in which each person integrates information from the external world;

(5) environmental evaluation, i.e., all the judgments made by the individual about the quality of different aspects, of the environment, aesthetic, hygienic, functional, and so forth; and

(6) attitudes to the environment—what the individual expects of his quality of life and the needs which that satisfies effectively.

Seven types of methods are used by researchers. Three are observational, one used simulation, and three rely on questioning. Each produces different data. Global observation (described as "holistic" by some authors) and the nondirective interview have been excluded since they seem to be best suited to use in the pilot stage as a way of refining hypotheses.

Discreet observation has the advantage that subjects do not know that they are being observed. It consists basically of the study of existing records (for example, crime statistics, complaints) and the investigation of how they may relate to the

TABLE 1.1   Methods and Data Types in Environmental Psychology

DATA TYPE

METHOD	Attitudes to the environment	Environmental evaluation	Environmental cognition	Non perceived effects of the environment on behavior	Perceived effects of the environment on behavior	Action on the environment
Discreet observation				X		X
Systematic observation				X		
Performance				X		
Factual questioning					X	X
Games	X		X			X
Attitudes and personality Questionnaires	X	X			X	
Indirect methods	X	X	X			

environment and be explained by the characteristics of particular sites.

Systematic observation relates to the case in which direct observation in the field is organized in such a way as to both gather data as objectively as possible and to be able to classify the information so as to facilitate statistical analysis. Barker is probably the originator of this method. He positioned trained observers at specific points. Each one took observations for 30 minutes and noted incidents or "behavior episodes" during that period. The sampling of the observation periods obviously varied according to the behavioral site chosen.

To try to make the observations more rigorous and less dependent upon the observer, the use of photographs which could be assessed by several judges has been proposed (Davis and Ayers, 1975). Ittelson et al. (1976) propose a more rigorous method yet in the behavioral mapping technique. Researchers who use this methodology compile an inventory of observable behaviors during a pilot study and classify them so as to produce a list of activity types. Observers are trained to record and classify these behaviors. It is therefore possible to compare data gathered in terms of sites, periods, or individuals. Winkel and Sasanoff (1976) have proposed tracking, using a grid which can describe in detail the movements of visitors to public spaces such as museums and from which the sequence of their movements can be reconstructed.

Observing *performance* consists of gathering information about the work-rate of subjects in different places, or about learning curves, academic progress, and so on. This type of data has predominantly been used in the laboratory to investigate the effects of physical conditions of work and the effects on communication networks of spatial layouts. These studies can, however, be carried out in the field. Glass et al. (1969) studied the relation between noise in dwellings and the scholastic performance of children. It must be borne in mind that each person's performance is determined by numerous factors, including motivation. The oldest work in this area is perhaps that carried out at the Hawthorne Works by Elton Mayo (Roethlisberger and Dickson, 1939). He clearly demonstrated that the physical conditions at work only had an effect on performance via the psychological meaning of the environment to the worker.

Another possibility for the psychological study of the environment is *questioning*. A great variety of information can be gathered in this way. Subjects can be asked to describe or report factual matters. It is simple, for instance, to give lists of activities to subjects and to ask them to indicate which are parts of their daily lives, or even which of them are subject to disturbance from environmental factors (Borsky, 1961). A more exact technique, still aimed at gaining factual information, is to ask each subject exactly how much time he has devoted to different activities, hour by hour, during a given period. The time-budget obtained in this way can be used to compare different groups or different periods, and also to answer such specific questions as the amount of time required by suburban and urban groups to carry out their shopping (Michelson and Reed, 1975). The motivation in the choice of a dwelling can be studied by questionnaire or interview (Canter et al., 1976) or even, indirectly, by a trade-off game (Robinson et al., 1975). In this case, subjects have to choose the characteristics of a house which they wish to acquire. As in "Monopoly" (the board game), each has a given amount of money to be used by the subject to buy various amenities and facilities (car parking, trees outside the windows, nearby shops), the prices of which are fixed. Putting it another way, the choice indicates an order or priority among the different possible elements of amenity. Obviously, the technique can be used to compare different groups of subjects.

Attitude questionnaires gather information about the needs and opinions of subjects in regard to different aspects of their environments. All the classical methods of attitude measurement can be used: adjective check-lists, Likert scales, scalograms, multiple-choice questionnaires, the Osgood semantic differential, and so forth. It should, however, be noted that the data at present available have not yet allowed us to proceed to factor analyses adequate for us to describe the major axes of environmental needs, attitudes, and evaluations. Work in occupational psychology on the structure of motivation and satisfaction already shows that such analysis is possible and that it facilitates comparative research.

Several questionnaires concern characteristics of the personality relating directly to environmental dispositions. McKechnie (1974) constructed an inventory of 184 items evaluating eight named personal dispositions: pastoralism, urbanism, environmental adaptation, stimulus-seeking, environmental trust, "antiquarianism," need for privacy, and mechanical orientation. Little (1972) constructed a questionnaire of orientation towards people and objects, which gave a four-category typology: object specialist, people specialist, generalist, and nonspecialist. Sonnenfeld (1969) is the originator of an environmental personality inventory which describes four factors: environmental sensitivity, environmental control, mobility, and environmental risk-taking. Marshall (1972) constructed a scale specifically intended to assess attitudes to privacy; and it must be recalled that Gough's (1965) personality inventory was validated in relation to different environmental behaviors.

All of the techniques mentioned are aimed at the analysis of aspects of man-environment relationships perceived by the subject or clearly visible in his behavior. There remain indirect methods which seek to show unconscious processes, at the level of attitudes, cognitions, and the structures which are implicit in attitudes. Projective tests have been used to construct an initial inventory of individual needs in the environment (Levy-Leboyer, 1977) and to analyze attitudes to natural catastrophes (Saarinen, 1973). Similarly, but using a verbal technique, Kelly's Role Construct Repertory Grid asks subjects to react to triads of elements (e.g., kitchen, drawing room, office) by indicating in which way two elements are similar but different from the third. This has the advantage of making the subject himself produce the constructs which he uses to perceive and evaluate the environment. Another similar method is that of cognitive mapping. This method provides information about how environments too big to be perceived instantaneously are represented. This was the method by which Lynch (1960) had the inhabitants of Boston, Jersey City, and Los Angeles make maps of the centers of their cities. The same method has been used in France by Chombart de Lauwe (1976) to describe town and country children's representations of space, and by Stanley Milgram and Denise Jodelet (1976) for Paris, which yielded a very picturesque collection of maps of Paris and a frequency table of the 50 most frequently mentioned elements. Any inhabitant of Paris reading this study will not be surprised to learn that the first five included the Seine, the Arc de Triomphe, Notre Dame, and the Eiffel Tower.

The methodological and theoretical survey above gives the impression, without a doubt, of an incomplete but dynamic body of thought still seeking to express its character. At the present time, environmental psychology, from the theoretical point of view, is at the "No" age. It can be defined by what it is not, having tried general models and found that they do not work. At the same time, researchers have borrowed methods of investigation from diverse branches of psychology (social, experimental, differential) and have tried to invent new ones. By so doing, environmental psychology exhibits its multivariate and interdisciplinary character. Each investigation is concerned simultaneously with physical, social, and psychological parameters. The broad lines of the new model are just beginning to emerge. Whether through aspects of theories or of methods, researchers have drawn one general conclusion: that there are no general laws for environmental effects. Environmental psychology must not therefore be reduced to an analysis of the external world and its psychological functions. The environment has, to be sure, environmental effects, but they are mediated by individual variables and interact with them. Two approaches are thus beginning to converge: (1) Observing environmental behaviors (man-environment systems) as wholes in order to understand their structure and organization; and (2) Analyzing the personal factors that transform the shared environment into the personal one—to understand how each person deciphers his environment, because this affective/cognitive representation is the source of intermediate variables determined both by the individual and his environment and which, in their turn, influence environmental behavior. This dual orientation explains why a large proportion of the fruitful studies in this field are concerned with perception and evaluation, the subject matter of the next chapter.

CHAPTER 2

Perception and Evaluation of the Environment

A visitor enters a classroom for the first time, the layout and decor of which a colleague wishes him to admire. "Are you aware of the special atmosphere of this room?" asks his guide. What does he reply? Does he describe the ventilation, the illumination, the temperature or the humidity? Or will he comment on the social atmosphere, the academic activity, or the staff-student relationships which should be encouraged in such a class? This ambiguity is very revealing. The same vocabulary can be used to describe the physical aspects of the environment and, in a way which is at the same time of greater significance and less precise, to define its psychological characteristics, by which I mean the global evaluation of the environment made by the person in it, as well as his opinions about the effects which that environment should have on the behavior of the people in it. Physical descriptions, aesthetic evaluations, personal preferences, predictions, and expectations mix together and interact. In addition, in perception as much as in evaluation, our visitor has recourse to his store of mental representations and cognitive schemas. He recognizes what he sees by drawing upon cultural norms about what a classroom should be like. And that is not all. Both his perception and his evaluation of the place follow from the dynamics of the context. If he had to teach in that room, he would evaluate it differently, depending upon what and whom he was going to teach.

In reality, all our modes of experience, perceptual, affective, and normative, are brought into action at the same time. For the passing traveller, for the person who is there, every environment is perceived simultaneously as a collection of specific properties (a mountain is high, a town is closed in, a room is small, the sky is blue, and so forth) which cannot be disaggregated and which has not only its own cognitive structure but also general qualitative features, as well as a particular appearance defined by adjectives such as "wild," "noble," "sad," "hot," or "oppressive." To put it another way, the perception of the physical features of the environment is inseparable from affective, aesthetic, and normative assessments, that is to say, from a *social* evaluation. This evaluation depends upon the perception of objects, but exceeds that perception in complexity and significance.

It is thus obvious that the perception of the environment is a great deal more than the sum of the perceptions of those objects which make up that environment. This is true even when the investigation of those perceptual processes which relate to the real environment must make use of results derived from the laboratory, studies of what one may call primary perception. Every attempt to analyze environmental perception must therefore change the nature of that perception. The only legitimate approach to it must be that of focusing the spotlight on one of the phases of the perceptual-evaluative process, without forgetting the modulating effects of other aspects. This situation provides environmental perception research with a particular set of features.

In the first place, these features have developed relatively recently, assuming as they do simultaneous treatment of a large number of different parameters. While the experimental study of perception has led to a considerable amount of research, reviewed in the recent works of Frances (1963), Piaget et al. (1963), and Reuchlin (1977), the perception of the real world has been a long-neglected field.

In the second place, the goals of studying the perception of the environment are quite specific. In studying the perception of objects in the laboratory, the perspective adopted is that of pure research aimed at the development of knowledge. On the other hand, environmental psychology has developed as an applied field dealing with concrete problems put by "clients." Clearly, this produces a loose structure which makes for difficulty in synthesis and review. In addition, it confers an interdisciplinary character upon this type of research. Quite often (and perhaps because of the difficulty of finding psychologists who are interested in their problems), specialists in other fields concerned with the environment have "borrowed" from psychologists this or that technique which seemed useful, and have applied it themselves in the field. In this way, a recent book edited by Ittelson (1973), himself a psychologist, had twelve co-authors: five psychologists, four architects, and three geographers. This multidisciplinary approach lends an undeniable richness to the articles, but it is difficult to master technically: very often, a method is utilized without well-structured hypotheses or precise research questions.

The third characteristic concerns the scatter of results, or, more exactly, individual differences in perception. In the laboratory, perceptual targets are varied systematically: for example, the complexity of the stimulus-figure is changed, or its symmetry, the presentation time, or even the familiarity of the stimulus to the subjects. This allows us, in a way, to dismantle the mechanisms of perception. It is clear, however, that all subjects do not respond in the same way. For example, consider Gibson and Walk's (1960) experiment. Children between 6 and 14 months of age, separated from their mothers by a plank, were encouraged by their mothers to cross the plank. This plank had an opaque covering on one side of it and a thick glass sheet on the other. Of the 27 children who crawled towards their mothers, 24 used the opaque route and only 3 crossed the glass. It can be deduced that there is an early perceptual awareness of the void below the glass. One baby in nine crossed the glass sheet, but the aim of the experiment was not to explain this minority behavior. In other studies, the perception of visual illusions has been compared in different age-groups: there are a large number of examples in the work of Piaget, as well as in the whole field of perceptual development. For example, Vurpillot (1974) had drawings of houses compared by children of different ages and was able to show that before 6 years of age, children did not consider that when something was moved or exchanged for something else that it was of any significance. The author does not, however, linger over the rare exceptions to this general rule.

It is only in the field of complicated perceptual conflicts that an individual typology is attractive. Witkin (1959) placed his subjects in a variable-angle chair, in a room which itself was not horizontal. In this situation, of course, the subjects received conflicting information about the vertical: incorrect visual information but correct proprioceptive information from the inner ear. This conflict was resolved in different ways by different subjects. Some were more "field-dependent" than others, and consequently it is realistic to talk about individual cognitive styles in this area. Even in this case, however, the observed differences between people were interpreted in terms of abstract personality features, and the analysis was not pursued any further. There was no attempt to look at the previous experience of the subjects which would encourage the differentiation of dominant cognitive styles or of specific attitudes toward the environment.

The same case does not apply when it is a matter of investigating either the natural or built environment. On the one hand, individual differences are facts of observation, but are not described as dependent variables that are resistant to analysis. In fact, it is not personality traits which explain the variance in perceptions, but the type of previous experiences or the store of mental representations built up as a result of the subject's activities. Introducing the idea of individual differences into the investigation of environmental perception emphasizes the way in which past experience determines present understanding. On the other hand, researchers want to take these differences into account in as systematic a way as possible since they have in view the optimization of the environment, which must be the adaptation of the environment to suit each individual. In addition, the scientific analysis of these differences represents an important part of environmental psychology. They permit the understanding of the continual interaction of the physical, psychological, social, and cultural aspects of the environment and give concrete meaning to the theoretical imperative that we must consider the environment as a whole and carry out holistic investigations.

The preceding remarks explain the plan adopted for this chapter. In the first place, an attempt is made to explain how the environment is perceived—or, more or less, what we know about the problem. Clearly, in this area it is difficult to separate laboratory research from that done in the field. For example, it is useful to observe spatial perception in the laboratory: such experiments frequently concern themselves with the processes of distance estimation. But even though observations are based on what has been found in the laboratory, the analysis is concerned with the way in which mental representations of a town are structured, by examining, for instance, the process of dealing with information overload, the subjective aspect of personal space, or even the sociocultural determinants of the personal mapping system that delimits the neighborhood.

In other words, in the laboratory perception is artificially isolated from that slice of life into which it is inserted. In the real environment, it is inseparable from current behavior and the individual who is acting. A town is not the same for the taxi driver working there, the tourist taking a walk, or the schoolchild who makes the same home-to-school journey every day.

Environmental evaluation, the subject of the second part of the chapter, is very closely linked to its perceptual elaboration, since there is no evaluation without identification. Conversely, evaluation (aesthetic, affective, and the like) structures and modifies both perception and mental representation. In the real world, there is a constant interaction between cognitive and normative processes. Nevertheless, it is possible to isolate them in order to study them. The research to be described identifies the dimensions of environmental evaluation as well as the psychological needs and the value-hierarchies which support that evaluation.

The perceptual mechanism is not the equivalent of a passive camera, which would give an image of greater or lesser quality, but physically exact and identical in every case. On the contrary, perception is an active process in which the whole individual is involved. In perceiving the environment, the perceiver constructs it, and the result of the perceptual elaboration is individual to each person. It is therefore not possible to separate the perception from the individual who is perceiving. In other words, environmental perception is not just a function of the information in the environment which constitutes the sensory stimulus. It is just as much a function of the individual and his relation to that environment. More precisely, of what does perceptual activity consist?

In essence, there are three processes: the individual sorts, judges, and deciphers. In fact, the information received is from a variety of sources and relates to all the sense organs. Cortical and infracortical processes filter that which is significant from that which is not. This significance is assessed as a function of individual attitudes, activities, and needs—i.e., of the person and, at the same time, of the situation in which he is. Further, each individual is in control of his attention and therefore (especially by eye-movements) of his field of exploration. Besides this, the information received can be contradictory or ambiguous. Thus, the relative sizes of two objects can indicate that they are at different distances or that they are in fact of different dimensions. Perception therefore implies a real piece of detective work in which experience and acquired schema play a dominant role. Finally, the perceptual activity of the individual is not restricted to filtering incoming information and resolving conflicts. These are functions which could be performed by a computer. In the final analysis, perceptual activity implies the identification of shapes and objects which give a meaning to the outside world.

The general picture given above is true for all perceptual activity, not just for that which is specific to the environment. But is there any sense in such a distinction? In fact, there could be no perceptual activity without something to perceive and, in a strong sense, this thing must belong to the environment. The difference between the specific study of environmental perception and the general investigation of perceptual activities is found elsewhere. Incoming information from the environment and the cognitive schema which allow us to interpret it are essential to adaptation and to the survival of man in his environment. From this point of view, perception cannot be understood except as an instance of human activity in the environment, as described in the preceding chapter. There have been quite a few studies within this perspective, but so far they have not given us an exhaustive theoretical model of the perception of the environment.

However, it is possible to embark on a theoretical synthesis since one already exists for a related problem, that of person perception, for which a review of a large body of work has recently been made by Hastorf et al. (1970). Understanding, interpreting, and predicting the behavior of others is as important for our social adaptation as our perception of the physical environment is for our environmental adaptation. It is now known how specific observations (mimicry, a physical characteristic, a way of speaking, an attitude) are interpreted and organized around central characteristics. First impressions of other people are formed in this way, and they are lasting; that is, they determine the interpretation of subsequent information and the prediction of other people's behavior, and thus control a person's own behavior in regard to the other.

Without lingering here over the detail of experiments concerned with person perception, it can be said that the results obtained allow the construction of a general model, although not a definitive one. The same does not apply to environmental perception, where research has developed unequally, with a great deal of work in some areas and complete gaps elsewhere. In fact, three types of research have been carried out, each corresponding to a specific methodology and particular comparisons. In the following pages, an attempt will be made to describe these studies and their main results, and to draw out, as a provisional model, the conclusions which they share.

The first type of research is closest to the laboratory. It is concerned with the progressive development of environmental perception in the child, most notably spatial perception. By looking at the parallels between the development of perceptual performance in the child and the development of other psychological features (in particular, cognitive and motor performance), it has proved possible to extract the conditions and processes of environmental perception. Studying the perceptual adaptation of those born blind who have recovered their sight after cataract operations has also given similar information. The second class of studies concerns, quite specifically, the perception of distance. It is likely that, as Canter (1977) has suggested, this field has been so popular with researchers (geographers, sociologists, and psychologists) because of the ease of quantification. It is simple to have someone estimate distances, compare these with reality, and then look for variables which can explain the observed differences. The third group of investigations is more oriented towards the cognitive aspect of perception. Exploring the mental representation of the environment is just as seductive as distance estimation, because the experimental data lend themselves so easily to analysis and comparison. Respondents of varied ages and origins are asked to represent, by means of a drawing, their district, their town, or even the whole world, as seen by them. These studies are intended to either explore psychosocial categories, for example, what is the psychological meaning of the concept of neighborhood? (Lee, 1968), or to resolve practical problems, e.g., what is the user's spatial representation of the Paris Metro? (Goledzinowski, 1976).

PERCEPTUAL PROCESSES

Research into the perceptual and cognitive development of the child is clearly greatly indebted to Piaget and the Geneva school. It is impossible to do justice here to this great body of experimental work. As well as the works of Piaget and Inhelder, one could also read Hart and Moore (1973), Laurendeau and Pinard (1968), and Vurpillot (1974).

Nevertheless, it is vital to recall the distinction drawn by Piaget between action space and representational space. The first of these, appearing at up to 18 months, is that space within which the child places the objects he sees and in which actions and movements take place. The second allows the internalization and representation of the environment. Each of these spaces can be described in terms of a different geometry. At first, the child's space is topological and makes use only of qualitative relationships (being adjacent, being separate, enveloping, continuing). Later, the child develops the capacity to conserve the shape of objects even if they are moved and therefore change in appearance. In other words, the child knows how to carry out a geometrical operation consisting of projecting a point in space onto a line or a surface. The child's space has therefore become projective, and then eventually Euclidian when he knows how to use matric relations and geometric concepts.

By means of a series of ingenious experiments, Piaget and Inhelder have shown how these successive stages are developed. One of these experiments bears directly upon the perception of the natural environment. Children from 4 to 12 years of age were shown a plasticine model of three mountains differing in size, color and the objects to be found on the mountaintops, the model being placed on a square board. The children sat on one side of the board and a doll was placed at any one of the other three sides. The child was then shown different graphical representations of the mountains and asked to choose those which corresponded with the successive viewpoints of the doll. Children below seven years of age always chose the picture which corresponded to what they themselves saw—even when they walked around the model and took the position of the doll. The points of view became differentiated in the age-range from 7 to 9 years: first the children distinguished between in front and behind, and then between left and right. But it was not until 9 or 10 that the child mastered the whole of the representation and was capable of "decentration," i.e., of integrating within one representation all the different perceptions which are linked with different positions. According to Piaget, moving from topological space to projective space is made possible by the subject's own mobility (movements constantly change perceptions and allow research into the constant factors which control environmental perception), as well as by the subject's activity (experimentation upon the environment and feedback from actions).

Bruner (1966) puts forward another conception of the role of action in perceptual development: "to the extent that action is goal-directed and is capable of changes in direction, it must be based upon a representation which is more than simple stimulus-response links." In other words, learning is at first based upon responses and then upon places, which could not come about without a mediating spatial representation. Bruner's ideas rest upon Mandler's (1962) experiment, in which blindfolded subjects had to learn to run a maze. When they performed without error, they were asked to continue the experiment and go through the maze again. This procedure differs from classic learning experiments, in which observation generally ceases after the first successful trial, but is more related to the conditions of everyday life: having learned a new route, we generally repeat it a number of times. Bruner observed that behavior changed under these conditions. Subjects proceeded according to a general picture of the maze and did not use any specific sequences of action. Habit, based on repetition, led to the behavior being dependent on representation.

Without wishing to enter into the debate between Bruner and Piaget (whether sensorimotor and cognitive representations are the same or different), it is still necessary to use the idea of the role of a behaviorally based representation with multisensory support in explaining observations made of people born blind but gaining sight after a cataract operation. Such people are immediately capable of distinguishing colors, but cannot identify distant objects because they are deprived of tactile information. Coordination of motor and visual experiences is essential to the construction of the representations necessary for complete perceptual development. Perceptual learning is therefore much more than a simple association between visual and tactile messages. It depends upon the interpretation of invariants, i.e., constant, conserved properties of objects, and upon the more or less exact way in which the individual represents to himself the effects of his own movements upon the environment he perceives.

The role of exploratory and other behavior in determining environmental perception has received little experimental attention in the adult. Ittelson et al. (1976), however, have carried out an ingenious piece of laboratory research in a specially constructed room at the City University of New York. This room had movable mirrors as well as unfamiliar acoustic and luminous environments. The subjects were introduced into the room without any particular instructions. All they knew was that they would be asked questions later. Their behavior was observed, and after 15 minutes they were questioned about the "environmental contingencies" of the room. The experimenter was in fact able to allow the subjects to control the sound and the illumination in the room, but the subjects had not been told which behavior allowed them this control. After analysis, the subjects' responses were put into two categories, according to whether they dealt with "experiential" descriptions—impressions, feelings—or "structural" descriptions, making reference to the physical characteristics of the room. In addition, the activity of the subjects was quantified together with the level of their awareness of the contingencies of the room—the modes of changing the different happenings in the room. The results showed a clear positive relation between the frequency of activity, the discovery of contingencies, and the type of description. Structural descriptions were associated with high levels of activity and discovery. Experiential descriptions were present when the level of activity was low and the contingencies ill-perceived. In addition, the authors pointed to the large scatter in behaviors and contingency—awareness. The number of activities varied between zero and 151 different activities in 15 minutes. In some cases, the subject never discovered that he could control anything, while in others the subject discovered all 8 contingencies within 15 minutes.

In summary, whether we are considering exploratory activities concerned with a large number of types of information and which therefore lead to the search for constants, or coordinated activities which require the performance of abstract operations, the role of behavior in the perception of the environment is clearly visible. In other words, representational schemata essential to useful environmental perception are built up in the course of cognitive development based on personal experience. This role for experience also seems to be the central theme, though from another point of view, of studies of distance perception and estimation.

DISTANCE PERCEPTION

The investigation of distance perception gives a clear indication of how contradictory information is handled and how perceptual decision-making uses various indices and gives them different weightings. The size of objects perceived in the environment can be interpreted as either a real difference in size or an indication of distance. More generally, landscape relief is seen as a function of the relative size of the objects in that landscape. These visual stimuli are thus sources of information, and the perceptual process depends on making a choice between several possibilities—a probabilistic decision. Let us consider the conditions of the choice. From the point of view of visual physiology, the perceiver can use information which has two characteristics. First, the eyes are at a distance from one another, which causes the two eyes to have different retinal images of the same object. In addition, the eyes converge to a greater or lesser extent depending upon whether the object is near or far. Further, there is the experience acquired of the relative size of familiar objects, which helps in assessing distance on the basis of apparent size.

Finally, Gibson (1966) has shown that texture density (the fineness of perceived detail in surface irregularities in, for instance, the paving of the road, the appearance of the ground, or the weave of a cloth) decreases with distance and therefore contributes to the registration of distance and the perception of relief.

Therefore, different information, sometimes coherent but often contradictory, is received by the subject and interpreted without any explicit or conscious reasoning. In addition, acquired knowledge is imposed upon sensory data. Pieron (1955) has shown that if the relief of a human face is reversed by changing over the photographs in a stereoscopic viewer, the normal perception is resistant to the change and the face is seen in the usual way.

The ability to rectify information is such that when people have worn, for experimental purposes, spectacles which invert visual images, they have adapted their perception to the circumstance. Brunswik (1956) developed a model of the perceptual process which fits in very well with what has just been described, and called the model the "perceptual lens." The environment scatters stimuli about, which the perceptual organs reassemble and reorganize just as a lens catches light rays. Reorganization obeys the principle which Brunswik has described as "probabilistic functionalism": the information is interpreted so that the perception makes the best bet possible. This perceptual activity is constantly checked against behavior, conferring upon it an "ecological validity." In one of his experiments, Brunswik accompanied a subject for a normal day and, at different times, asked her to estimate the size and distance of different objects in her environment. He was able to show that the correlation between objective physical measurements and the estimations made by the subject was quite low. The perceptual synthesis, however, was quite exact. By combining inexact information, the subject expressed a general perception of the environment which was valid and well-suited to her needs.

Ames (1951), by creating extremely ingenious trick interiors, showed how the choice was made between different possible interpretations of the size of objects. He built a room with non-parallel walls and a sloping floor, in which the back wall had two unequally-sized windows. The subject was only able to see the interior by monocular vision, without being able to move the useful eye or to touch anything inside the room. In these artificial conditions, two people of the same size, one placed at the highest point of the floor and the other where the room had the greatest height, were perceived as a dwarf and a giant. As soon, however, as the subject could move his eye or examine the field with the aid of a stick, the perceptual error was immediately corrected.

With the exception of the work of Ittelson, the studies just cited antedate environmental psychology as it is properly understood. Investigations of distance in the field have since been carried out, starting from the approach used in the laboratory, in essence by comparing physical measurements with the subjective appraisal of two points in the environment—in different situations or with different subjects. It has been possible to work in the real environment as it is lived in while still being able to use quantified data. This has allowed questions like the following to be investigated: Which conditions and factors lead to overestimation, underestimation, or correct answers? Are estimates relatively more exact when dealing with short or long distances? Clearly, the factors responsible for over- and underestimation can just as easily concern the individual (his experience and his activities) as the environment (structure and configuration). In fact, the existing research has brought out three groups of determinants: the structure of the environment, the behavior of the subject making the estimate, and affective aspects of the man-environment relationship.

Briggs (1973) investigated the distance estimates made by geography students at the University of Ohio. All the points between which the distance had to be estimated were related to Columbus, the town in which the university stood. The central hypothesis of the study was that there would be overestimation of distances towards the town center, for a number of reasons: the traffic there is heavier, there are more crossings to slow down pedestrian and motorist, and especially because there are many more points of interest such as buildings, monuments, shop-windows, and crossroads which can draw the attention and break up distance. There is of course a parallel with time estimation, since durations seem longer when they are divided up into discontinuous activities. The experimental results confirmed the author's hypothesis: journeys towards the center were more frequently overestimated, and those from the center more often underestimated. However, Lee (1970) had observed that students at his university (Dundee, Scotland) overestimated distances outward from the center, thus justifying Brennan's Law (1948), according to which housewives have a greater tendency to use shops sited between their homes and the town center rather than those situated away from the center, even if the latter were nearer home. These contradictory findings are probably explained by differences between the samples. As Stringer (1975) has remarked, students recently transplanted into a university town have habits which vary in their fixity. In addition, both Lee's and Briggs's work make use of different explanations within their hypotheses. The viability of these explanations has not been studied in an independent or exact way in the course of the experiment.

It is this task which Canter (1971, 1974) and Canter and Tagg (1975) have set themselves, by showing which elements of the urban structure are responsible for the estimation of distance. They observed, in several cities, the existence of subjective barriers. When the estimation was concerned with a journey which crossed these barriers, the distance was exaggerated. In London, distances between points on either side of the Thames or to the south of the river were more frequently overestimated than those north of the river. This overestimation is possibly based on a spatial representation of urban rivers which tends to reduce their curves and meanderings, with similar smoothing having been observed in Paris by Milgram and Jodelet (1976). Barriers, however, are not only geographical obstacles, they can also be the gaps in the transport system. Canter observed in Tokyo that distances were overestimated in areas not served by the subway system. In London, distances between points served by *different* subway lines were more often overestimated than those along a given line. Similar studies in Glasgow, Edinburgh, Heidelberg, and Nagoya have shown in just the same way that distance overestimation is linked to urban complexity and to the presence of a central river. These studies also show how interesting it would be to go further into the psychological meanings of barriers and nodes. Such an analysis would probably show the varying significance of the environment for different individuals, together with the individual experience of the places lived in. Among these experiences, by which the individual learns about his environment by what he does in it, it is clear that the mode of transport is of special importance. Starting in 1957, Lee investigated how the environmental representations of rural children were affected by the way in which they travelled to school. Teachers made 883 assessments of how well children got on at school, and these were correlated with the time it took for them to get to school. Disturbance in the children increased as a function of increased journeytime, but the relationship was very different among children who walked and those who came by other means. The latter were in general more disturbed, even though their journeys took less time. Lee explained this by suggesting that the child who lived a long way from the school constructed two representations of his environment (i.e., separate ones from school and home) which were heterogeneous. For the walker, there would be clear links between the two representations. But for the child on the bus, these links would be weak. The bus would use an impersonal route and go away when the child was at school, cutting him off physically from the home to which he could not return by his own efforts.

It must be noted how cognitive and affective factors are intermingled in the process, as well as adaptive and representational effects. More recently, Canter (1971) interviewed people who lived in London and compared their estimates of distance in relation to the mode of transport they used and where they lived. Distance estimates were of about the same degree of accuracy in bus users and non-users; regular tube users underestimated distances; and the farther from the center that respondents lived the more they underestimated the length of their journeys. In short, even if the mechanisms and agents of the distortion are not always clear, it is nonetheless obvious (as observed by Battro and Ellis, 1972; Lowrey, 1971; and Pailhous, 1970) that the experience of urban space acquired by the individual is a function of learning and activity and, in particular, of the habitual routes taken by the individual around his town. It is just as clear that the representations acquired by experience and behavior determine perceptual judgments.

The factors mentioned above are essentially cognitive in nature. In fact, one wonders which affective factors enter into familiarity. Lee, for example, brings both into play when he mentions students' interest in the town center and the private learning of the children who go to school on foot. The classical research suggests that the value of objects affects the manner in which they are perceived. Bruner and Goodman (1947) showed that poorer children overestimated the size of coins. Beloff and Beloff (1961) showed that faces on photographs are perceived as close if they are the faces of the familiar and the liked. Very few studies have looked at the impact of valence on environmental perception, probably because, as Canter (1971) has remarked, it is rather difficult to measure valence. There are, however, studies which treat cognitive and affective factors as indivisible: those concerned with the size of the neighborhood for different subjects. In the first of these studies, Terence Lee had more than 200 housewives draw "their neighborhood" on a map of the Cambridge area. Analysis of the diagrams showed that subjective landscapes could be divided into three types:

(1) the neighborhood made up of the totality of social relationships;
(2) the homogeneous neighborhood, including all the people belonging to the same group and living in the same way as the respondents;
(3) the neighborhood unit in a sense very close to that used by the town planner.

In addition, Lee constructed a quantifiable index, the *neighborhood quotient,* which is the ratio between the number of houses, shops, and blocks of flats which are included in the area of the neighborhood and the total of all of these in the locality. This index allows us to describe how the environment is perceived from an affective and social point of view—the extent to which the individual feels himself to be included in the community. It would be interesting to use this diagnostic tool as a systematic correlate of the objective characteristics of the environment.

THE REPRESENTATION OF THE ENVIRONMENT

All of the studies which have been cited as examples show how the meaning of the concept environment has progressively broadened. Investigating in the laboratory how distances are estimated by a fixed observer looking at a stationary landscape (or possibly a model) allows the analysis of the sensory and cognitive aspects of perception, the way in which they are developed, integrated, and based upon personal experience. Analyzing distance and the factors explaining over- and underestimation of distance is, however, a radically different approach. For the subject, it is no longer a matter of saying how far away from him an object in his visual field is, but of imagining the distance he would have to travel if he were to go from one place to another, from one town to another, for example. This evaluation of distance is strongly influenced by affective factors, more specifically by the belonging relation which is woven by habit and familiarity. It can be seen, as Lundberg et al. (1972) remark, that subjective distance also has affective consequences. It determines, exponentially, the emotional reverberation of distant events. The greater the perceived distance between where a person lives and another town, the less a person feels himself involved in what goes on there.

To perceive separation is to perceive the distance relative to a fixed point; but perceiving distance is perceiving an operative environment. Describing a neighborhood expresses social and emotional belonging and the way in which a person places himself into it as an active behaving person, socialized in a community and a habitat. In making a representation of the external environment, a further step is taken. The *mental map* can be used to study how the relation between the individual and the outside world leads to a synthesis of the physical and the psychological. Studying the representations which the individual makes, not only of the environment which he can take in at a glance, but also of a much larger world, restores to the words "far" and "near" their triple sense of physical distance, relatedness, and chosen relationship (near to town, a near relation, close in ideas).

The idea of using mental maps to study environmental and perceptual representation comes from Kevin Lynch, whose book (Lynch, 1960), although criticized at some length, introduced an experimental tool which has been used by many psychologists and geographers wishing to analyze representations of the external world. This method makes use of the idea that every person has a map "in his head," indeed, many maps, at different scales. Kaplan (1973) states that the ability to represent the environment mentally is a condition for survival and one of the bases of natural selection, to the extent that it increases perceptual efficiency since the cognitive schemata which are implied reduce perceptual ambiguities. From this point of view, the mental map is in essence a summarized and juxtaposed representation of the sequence of actions constituting the ways used to get from one point to another. The mental map is at the same time a condition for perception and the result of personal experience of action and movement in the environment, and for this reason is an interesting source of data for the psychological investigation of perception of the external world.

However, as Canter (1977) states, the mental map obtained by asking a subject to draw his town, his district, or his country is not a simple piece of information. The ability to draw what is represented varies. More specifically, the act of drawing a map implies four activities which are not forcibly brought into action when the "map in the head" is used in real life to organize journeys and to allow the recognition of routes. The process of map drawing in fact assumes:

(1) the capacity to orientate oneself in space, i.e. to coordinate the relationships between the points represented and the points on the map;
(2) the ability to miniaturize a large space so as to contain on one sheet of paper a district, a town, or a country;
(3) some possibility of producing geometric projections; and finally
(4) knowledge of cartographic symbols: a line for a road, a cross for a church, and so on.

When the mental maps produced by different subjects are examined, it must be remembered that what is being studied is both the mental representation and the techniques of representing it on paper. It is thus the result of a double transformation: personal experience has been built up into the shape of mental representation, and the mental representation is expressed as a map in two-dimensional space.

Despite these reservations, the significance of mental maps is obvious. They allow all sorts of comparisons to be made: over time, in order to clarify the way in which perceptual experiences change the representation (Canter, 1977); between subjects who differ in social origin, sex, or nationality (Maurer and Baxter, 1972; Heinemeyer, 1967) to show how different ways of living affect mental representation. Generally speaking, these comparative studies are directed at two problems: first, the nature and process of cognitive elaboration and the role of experience in this; and second, the use to the individual of mental representations.

In fact, even though they contribute significantly to our orientation, mental representations are poor approximations of the external world. As Canter (1977) has remarked, mental maps are simplified images of reality. In support of his comment, Canter (1977) cites the study by Pocock on geography students (who should, of course, be used to maps) questioned about the vicinity of their university, with which they were all familiar. Each student was shown a drawing of a building (for example, the science building) and given its name. They were then asked to complete the sketch by drawing in a route and the appropriate road crossings. The results obtained showed quite clearly that even with skilled, informed subjects, the crossings were stylized and shown at right angles even when this was not the case, curves were straightened out (sometimes to the extent of becoming straight lines), and the routes were generally simplified.

Other studies which were also cited by Canter (Goodchild, 1974; de Jonge, 1962) supported the same interpretation. De Jonge, in commenting upon representations of the Hague, noted that his respondents did not have an internal map with coordinates ready to put down on paper. In reality, they had recorded fragmented plans of action which allowed them to find their way, but which lacked elements of continuity and exact details. In much the same way, when Sperandio (1975) studied signposting in a town by observing how visitors used information, he found that they started out by seeking key points and then, from these key points, looked for secondary objectives. Pailhous (1970) has described the hierarchic networks of traffic routes which constitute the taxi driver's representation of urban space.

This simplification is used elsewhere to facilitate the user's self-localization, particularly in the maps of subway systems, which ignore curves and acute angles so as to provide a schematic representation of what is underground. There is, of course, nothing surprising in this case in the fact that what is underground (shown schematically) does not correspond to the mental representation of the surface, which the traveller elaborates as a result of his experience as a pedestrian. Goledzinowski (1976) has remarked upon the way in which the subway map acquired by the traveller develops an autonomy in relation to the town.

The mental representation of the environment is at the same time an abstraction and a synthesis brought about from experience, repeated perception, and movements within the environment. However, the empirical nature of the information which is its basis, and the fact that the criteria of efficacy are behavior and affective orientation, condemn it to a lack of exactness. Appleyard (1973) summarized this useful imprecision by saying that our representation of the city is disjointed: "It is not an entity in the way in which the use of words such as schema or image would make one think." It is, rather, by its very nature incomplete and inexact. In addition, environmental representation is nonveridical since it is based upon scattered information which is badly organized and partial (Bruner, 1957). Canter (1977) showed, by an observational technique as simple as it was ingenious, how this mental representation is built up. He went to meet Nick, a young American, at London Airport. Nick had not been to England before. Canter asked him to draw a map of London before his visit, after a day there, after having lived in London for a week, and then after three weeks. Comparison of the maps showed how the number of identifiable points increased first (Parliament, Westminster, Hyde Park, Victoria Station, and the like), and then came the links between these points (Oxford Street, Piccadilly, Paddington, Euston Road, and so forth).

What are these mental maps made of? This problem was first raised by Lynch, and the classification which he proposed remains a tool of choice in the analysis of representations of urban space.

In his pilot study dating from 1960, Lynch had samples of the inhabitants of three different cities (Boston, Los Angeles, and

Jersey City) draw and describe their cities. In his analysis, Lynch defined five fundamental elements used to structure the representation of the city: *paths* which provide the links between one point and another; *edges* which represent the frontiers between parts of the city which have a distinct existence; *landmarks,* such as buildings, statues, parks, and the like which are identifiable places, remarkable enough to serve as the basis of a general orientation within the town. *Nodes* are points of transition from one activity to another: railway stations, airports, important road junctions. Finally, *districts,* which are reasonably large areas, homogeneous in character. This classification has been used in many studies since, and its advantages are indisputable. It is just as good for studying the origin of representations as for comparing them in relation to physical or social parameters.

It should always be remembered that mental representation varies with the type of environment. Francescato and Mebane (1973) used Lynch's classification to study the way in which the inhabitants perceived Milan and Rome, and showed that the frequency of the elements which make up the representation was the same in both cities (paths were the most frequent, then landmarks, nodes, districts, and edges). However, the subjects were aware of the specific character of each of the cities: the hills, the river, and the historic quarter of Rome, the radial arrangement of streets and the city center of Milan. Furthermore, the representation varied according to age, social class, and whether or not the respondent was born in that city. Daily experience of the city determined the image produced and, quite specifically, there was a strong influence from social experiences, such as friendship networks and the organizations to which people belonged.

Orleans (1973) compared representations of Los Angeles among subjects belonging to different social groups and showed that respondents with the widest social contacts were capable of making a representation of the whole Los Angeles region, while those with a more restricted social life only had a clear picture of a limited part of the megalopolis, perhaps only a few blocks. Milgram and Jodelet (1976) observed similar patterns of differences in the familiarity and identification of landmarks with their sample. Saarinen (1973), more ambitiously, compared differences in the way students from the United States and different European countries represented the world. They noted how many different factors were taken into account in the representations, and the inexactitudes and distortions which affected them, not just in terms of proximity to the place of residence, but also of the distinct shape of the country which catches the eye on the map, cultural factors giving a distant region a certain familiarity, and the news items which bring maps of the area into the newspapers. In this case, the experience of the environment is not direct, but is based on the frequency and richness of the digested information which appears in the media.

Briefly, perceptual experience permits the construction of mental representations of the environment which are diagrammatic, discontinuous, and distorted but still sufficient for the role they have to play in man-environment relations: orientation, finding the way, recognizing where you are, and moving to where you want to be. From this point of view, the study of mental maps completes the investigations already described by showing how perception is built up on the basis of past experiences, how these experiences are in some way stored in the form of mental representations, and implicit schemata which the experimenter can have made concrete as spatial images or possibly as verbal information about distance, neighborhood path and so on.

It must be noted, however, that the affective dimension is almost entirely absent from this account of environmental perception. This does not resemble reality. A simple survey carried out by Franck, Unseld, and Wentworth (described by Ittelson et al., 1976) allows us to see the constant interaction of different psychological levels. By using depth interviews, private diaries, and mental maps, these investigations secured an account of the experiences of students who had recently moved to New York. During the first eight months of their stay there, there was clear evidence of the active and creative nature of their environmental experience. The newcomer did not become adapted to his new conditions of life passively: "he actively chooses and utilizes certain opportunities from the range which he perceives. It is through these decisions and through his actions that the individual creates his experience of the new environments. The experiences he has will affect, in turn, his subsequent decisions and actions as well as his perception of what opportunities are available" (Ittelson et al., 1976: 196). Before deciding on their departure for New York, the students had weighed the pros and the cons of that decision. When they arrived, they had actively explored their new environment, and the data gathered showed that the quantity of exploratory behavior (questioning, walking about, deliberate visits, inspection of maps, attempting to learn the transport system, and attempting to become familiar with the area) was greater the more they had felt that they knew little about their new environment. These activities had two types of outcome. At first they learned to orientate themselves and to know where they were in a new environment. After this, concern with finding the way was no longer dominant and the attitudes of the person to the environment changed; in particular, they developed more confidence.

The authors made several other interesting observations. The majority of the group who were questioned indicated that life in New York was a source of tension and stress. They did not submit to this stress and tension passively, but actively constructed a series of behavioral adaptations: safety precautions, efforts to develop the positive aspects of urban life and to increase the time and energy devoted to friendship activities. Additionally, they all indicated that they had had specific attitudes and expectations (most frequently negative ones) about life in New York. These weighed upon their thoughts at the start of their stay in New York, manifesting themselves as anxiety and a tendency to stay at home. These fears were often shown to be unjustified, although sometimes valid. What was experienced became closely linked to decisions and actions. Expectations are constantly confirmed or rejected so that the emotional state and the basis for behavior are always changing. Expectations, emotional tone, the perception of environmental contingencies, and the principles behind behavior are woven together to create a complex and changing environmental experience.

The same study showed that another aspect of environmental

experience, the feeling of "being at home," was the result of a whole series of constituents: personalization of the dwelling, identifying with it and having the sense of ownership, as well as having got to know the place. Finally, and perhaps most important, the whole process of exploration, action, and perception of the new environment seemed to modify the newcomer's attitude toward himself. The old (French) saying that "travel shapes youth" was thus supported. Young people in the study said that this experience had developed their personalities, that their views of their own self-sufficiency had improved, and that their horizons had been broadened, but at the same time they had become more cynical and suspicious.

FROM PERCEIVING TO EVALUATING THE ENVIRONMENT

As Ittelson has remarked, a new environment can be perceived affectively, but so can an environment which has been forgotten but revisited. From this point of view, it can be stated that perception and representation of the environment, the maps which everybody constructs in their heads, and the constant interactions between expectations and reality are all at the same time cognitive and affective. This qualitative, personal dimension has been seen as especially important in environmental evaluation.

The relationship between perception and evaluation of the environment is very much a functional one. Kaplan (1973) clearly described the four levels of knowledge of his environment which a person needs in order to be capable of surviving. First, he has to know where he is, and this with some exactness, rapidly and error-free. In spite of the ambiguities in the incoming information, which we have discussed, it is very often impossible for a person to "give himself the luxury of a second glance" (Bruner, 1957). Mental representation plays a key role in perceptual decoding. Second, a person must be capable of predicting what is going to happen next—that is, to connect the present representation with future ones. Third, prediction is not sufficient to make a decision. An evaluation must accompany it, made in relation to the value judgments of the individual. Action represents both the end of a process and the last phase of mental representation: it can just as easily be the object of internal representation as objects or events in the environment. Thus, the maps which respondents draw in experimental studies, and the cognitive representation of which they are the manifestation constitute, simultaneously, both a generalization of perceptual experiences and the concrete expression of a structure of motives, a structure which integrates projection into the future (Kaplan, 1973). A person can only envisage the future if he is in possession of adequate mental representations. Mental maps reflect the four aspects of knowing—perception, generalization, motivation, and projection into action—in their distortions and errors.

The way in which people represent their environment corresponds to basic needs. Lynch was the first to put forward a description of the psychological functions involved in mental representations of the environment by developing two notable themes: (1) the clarity and significance of the environment; (2) the mystery connected with coherence. When the environment is constructed so as to be clearly *readable,* when it can easily be imaged, then, according to Lynch, it furnishes cognitive support to the idea of a social community and in this way gives a feeling of security to the individual. This social and affective function of the city has been the subject of investigation by a geographer (Wood, 1971) working in Mexico. He was able to show that the city of San Christobal fulfilled this social function very well because of specific physical characteristics. The same structures were in fact found at three levels (the house, the district or *barrio,* and the town), which enabled the use of the same type of mental representation for all three, facilitating the integration of perceptual experiences. Each level, for instance, possessed a completely common space: the patio for the house, the square for the barrio, and the central *zocolo*. Religious observance had a dedicated space at each level: the family shrine, the barrio church, and the cathedral. This structural repetition represented the vehicle for environmental legibility and guaranteed the individual's integration with the nested social units of the family, the district, and the town. It is possible to put these observations into the context of those made from the perspective of individual differences concerning cognitive complexity.

It is well-known that the record of concepts and abstract dimensions varies widely from one individual to another. This is also true of the environment. The number of cognitive dimensions available to an individual for the evaluation of his environment—that is, his ability to discriminate different aspects of it—is a representation of a personality characteristic. It has been shown that cognitive complexity is correlated with overall satisfaction with the environment (Canter, 1970). It is perhaps the case that there is no such general need for an imageable, legible environment, but for an environment the complexity of which corresponds to the individual capacity to collect information and process it. Lynch has also supported the idea that the image of the city should give the individual inhabitant both mystery and coherence. Mystery comes from the development of "the intensity of human experience" from the deep meaning of the city (both direct and indirect). Coherence is necessary because a person requires an environment, the structure and meaning of which display neither ambiguity nor inconsistency.

Lynch's statements are made a priori, on the basis of a number of observations far too small to support his hypotheses. There is, however, great merit in raising the problem of the functions of the environment and therefore of the needs which the built environment must satisfy, and in suggesting that these needs go beyond those of the physical necessities of shelter, warmth, and the requirements of family and social life. This area poses an important problem in psychology to the architect and the town planner. If we wish to create an environment adapted to those in residence, it is necessary to know exactly what needs should be satisfied by that environment. This is a problem with several facets. Looking back on this chapter, it is easy to see that a list of problems has been introduced, all of which are closely linked with the others. The review began with the perception of objects in the external world, of their distance, separation, and so on. Then we posed the problem of their identification, the storage and use of past experience, and the representation of the environment. This representation is subjective, distorted, dominated by affective factors. This is the problem of evaluation. In short, it is not possible to examine separately the problem of what is perceived from that of what gives rise to satisfaction.

In reality, it is necessary to approach this double question at different levels. The first level is conceptual: how are the qualities of the environment perceived? Clearly, this problem is not only a cognitive one. It is one thing to say that this room is large or bright, this wall is yellow or dirty, and quite another to feel impressions of happiness, privacy, or safety which are produced by just those rooms, walls, or colors. It would therefore be useful to add psychological concepts (comfortable, welcoming, private) to the concrete characteristics based in the physical sciences and used to describe environments (large, quiet, bright), and to investigate the relations between them. What is needed is to raise specific questions such as these: is privacy perceived independently of warmth and comfort, or is there a cluster of closely linked factors? What produces feelings of comfort? Household appliances? Soft chairs? Absence of noise?

AN EXAMPLE: THE PERCEPTION OF ENVIRONMENTAL RISK

There has been very little research on this topic. What there is has often approached the topic indirectly, by means of social investigations of natural disasters carried out by geographers, notably those at the universities of Toronto and Chicago. The tendency for inhabitants returning after a natural disaster (such as an earthquake, flood, tornado) to go back spontaneously to the same place has been known for a long time. Burton (1972) gives three reasons for this: the objective advantages of these regions (for example, they are often fertile); the natural passivity of individuals who could not overcome the difficulties of moving to another region; and underestimation of the risks. It is this last point which is of interest to us: how is risk perceived and evaluated? Kates (1962) interviewed people resident in two different areas recently affected by serious floods. Many of them did not believe that there was a serious risk of another flood, an illogical belief in the sense that they were aware these events had been repeated in the past. Burton et al. (1968) made the same observation and classified the attitudes related to this optimism according to two frameworks. Either the respondents denied the risk by declaring that it would not happen again (lightning doesn't strike twice in the same place), or they reduced the risk by emphasizing the rarity of the event and their confidence in the protection granted them by God or the government. Golant and Burton (1969) showed that risk is more underestimated among respondents who have themselves been victims of disaster. Saarinen (1966) observed the same general optimism among farmers in arid regions. He also used projective techniques (pictures inspired by the TAT) to investigate the attitudes of his subjects toward the risk of drought. The respondents were seen to be greatly disturbed, and the disaster had produced in them an intellectual confusion which made them passive. Under these circumstances, they were more proud of being able to endure difficult conditions than of being able to look for solutions or strategies which would avoid the danger. The inhabitants of dangerous regions therefore interpret reality so as to build for themselves a feeling of safety which does not rely on any objective analysis of the situation.

ENVIRONMENTAL QUALITIES

Following another set of ideas, researchers have attempted to show the subjectivity of environmental perception. Certain colors are often said to be "warm" (red, orange, yellow) and others "cold" (blue, green). Bennett and Rey (1972) tried to examine experimentally the way in which the color of a room could influence the feeling of comfort in its occupants. Subjects in a room, the temperature and humidity of which were controlled, had to wear spectacles with, successively, red, blue, and neutral lenses. Within each condition, the temperature was systematically varied and the subjects asked to assess their thermal comfort. The results showed that the color of the lenses did not affect

the assessment, but there was an "intellectual" relation between the color and warmth, since the subjects averred that the
"warm" colors were more conducive to warmth than the others.
Acking and Küller (1972) set themselves the same problem but
asked their subjects to evaluate, by means of a list of adjectives,
a set of photographs of rooms in which the color of the walls had
been systematically varied. The assessment of the social status
of the occupant was a function of the brightness of the room: the
darker the room, and the more laden with detail, the more subjects judged it as expensive and giving an impression of wealth.
Spaciousness increased with the lightness of colors, and the
impression of space was also increased if the intensity of the
colors of details was increased while the walls remained pale.
However, preferences for particular photographs differed between subjects, with no group tendency for any particular color
scheme emerging.

Flynn et al. (1973) approached the problem in a more original
way, by factor analyzing the responses on semantic differential
scales of subjects placed in a conference room with six successive
different lighting schemes. Five independent factors emerged:
an overall evaluation, perceptual clarity, spatial complexity,
spaciousness, and formality. These results at first seem rather
commonplace, but gain in interest when each factor is related by
the author to the different physical parameters that characterized the lighting schemes. For example, the second factor (perceptual clarity) was correlated with the luminosity of the conference table. In addition, each factor possessed a different
ability to make distinctions: spaciousness, for example, yielded
distinctions between all six schemes. Lighting conditions thus
influenced the overall perception of the room, and certain of the
physical characteristics determined specific psychological evaluations. The network of relationships was not obvious, however,
and only a mathematical analysis of the responses could give a
concrete meaning to the qualitative psychological evaluations.

From the same general perspective, Wools and Canter (1970)
investigated the factors which contribute to the impression that
a room is "friendly." The angle of the ceiling, the size of windows,
and the type of furniture were used as experimental variables.

Two levels of each variable meant there was an experimental design with eight conditions, each represented by a photograph of a model. The differences in the assessments made by means of a series of adjective pairs and intended to measure the friendliness of a room were constant over different experimental groups. The furniture was a major variable, followed by the ceiling angle, and the size of windows had no effect. These variables did not interact.

Other analyses have been carried out on the overall evaluation of the environment. This was the aim of the studies carried out at Berkeley by Craik and Zube (1976), who developed Perceived Environmental Quality Indices (PEQI) and undertook a major program of research to investigate the meaning and structure of these indices. Carl Axel Acking, one of whose studies of the assessment of the built environment has been reported above, has continued his work in this field. An architect working at the University of Lund (Sweden) in collaboration with psychologists, he has had subjects evaluate series of photographs of external scenes and interiors on semantic scales. Factor analysis of the resulting data has yielded eight factors in perception: acceptance, social status, closedness, individual character, complexity, affection, unity, and power. Lowenthal and Riel (1972) also used adjective pairs but had their subjects describe a place in which they had actually walked, in fine weather or in rain. The data were analyzed according to place and group of subjects. They also analyzed the way in which words were used by different subjects, and showed how much the meaning of some concepts varied between different groups: "nature," for example, had widely different meanings, indeed contradictory ones, for different subjects.

This type of research shows clearly that the concepts which can be used to describe the physical world are not adequate when it comes to defining the environment from a psychological point of view. There are two reasons for this: first, that the system of ideas defined precisely in physics does not correspond directly to the system of ideas used by psychologists. There are dimensions which emerge from scientific and objective observation which psychological assessment confuses. Second, physical concepts do not exhaust the psychological reality of the environment, since they do not take into account impressions such as those of warmth, privacy, unity, and the distinctiveness of the environment. We therefore need to pursue research which will identify the independent dimensions by which the environment is apprehended and assessed, as well as interdisciplinary studies which show how physical parameters determine environmental perception from a psychological point of view.

SATISFACTION AND THE ENVIRONMENT

The second problem which can be raised on the topic of environmental evaluation is more directly related to the quality of the environment: What determines individuals' satisfaction with their environment? Do specific satisfactions exist or is there a universal satisfaction? Do specific satisfactions and dissatisfactions interact? What are the psychological correlates of the concepts of annoyance and nuisance often mentioned in matters of noise and pollution?

One way of studying this problem is to define the objectives of environmental planning and then to investigate the users' satisfaction in relation to these aims. A series of such studies, concerned with national parks, have been carried out in the United States. These parks are, according to Proshansky, the counterpart to Americans of the European approach to ancient towns and monuments, and are intended to allow people to appreciate the beauty of landscapes untouched by man and to have direct contact with nature. It would be impossible to cite here every survey which has been carried out, but the more revealing problems can be discussed. Some studies have been restricted to producing a list of the facilities for users and an evaluation of their success in satisfying those users (for example, Shafer and Thomson, 1968). Other studies have displayed more depth, investigating the types of landscape preferred by visitors. Calvin et al. (1972) used the semantic differential technique to show, not unexpectedly, the importance of the beauty of the landscape. A second finding was more surprising: the respondents were appreciative of the "natural force," by which was meant the dynamic character of the landscape as it is perceived with all the senses, the noise and the scents as well as the visual information. There were other features attracting the visitor to these national parks, notably solitude, which was cited as "very important" by 82% of the visitors to the parks investigated by Stankey (1972). It is not clear, however, what was meant by solitude, since the majority of respondents came in groups: they did not want to meet other groups, particularly large ones; they accepted the idea of coming across other walkers but wished to camp alone; they accepted nonpolluting modes of transport (e.g., canoes) but not motor-boats (Lucas, 1964); they did not wish to find such signs of other groups as the remains of campfires or refuse.

Heimstra (1974), in his analysis of the results of studies in national parks, asks the central question: What do those who use these parks understand by "wilderness"? What does the experience of it do for them? According to Shafer and Mietz (1969), the answer is first, aesthetic satisfaction, then emotional and physical satisfaction, and finally, social satisfaction. According to Litton (1972), the characteristics of the natural environment which contribute to aesthetic satisfaction are the unity and harmony of the landscape, its vitality, vividness, and variety.

These satisfactions are obviously not the same for everybody, even if "everybody" is taken to refer to the groups of which visitors to national parks consist. Ciccetti (1972) and Cotton (cited by Proshansky) posed the same question and produced some results which disagree. Both of these writers suggest that the taste for wilderness is stronger at higher educational levels. Ciccetti, however, observed higher commitment to the preservation of nature in people brought up in the country or in small towns, while Cotton showed that it was people who were brought up in towns rather than those from the country who attached greater importance to "natural" values. As Heimstra notes, this is probably explained by the fact that the users of national parks come to them with different needs. This is, of course, all the more reason for making up an inventory of the real sources of satisfaction not limited to the hypotheses of a minority elite of decision-makers about what the majority are looking for in national parks and what contact with nature means to them.

The built environment presents the same sort of problems and should produce the same sorts of studies, but with two specific characteristics. On the one hand, a building has numerous purposes, some of which may be contradictory (for instance, quiet and proximity to transport). On the other, the growth of cities, producing megalopolises, frequently unplanned and undisciplined, has more often produced nuisance than satisfaction. It is this, perhaps, which explains the fact that the majority of studies concern specific aspects of the environment, even furniture. These fragmentary studies bear only upon the specific conditions under which they were carried out, since every environmental factor is evaluated in relation to all the others. It is exactly this network of interactions which we need to understand in a precise way. We learn nothing, however, about the evaluation process by reading the results of such opinion surveys as those of Fried and Gleicher (1961) or Zehner (1972), which describe the reasons for satisfaction with the environment given by those living in a particular district. The conclusions from these surveys were related to shared places: residents were content (or not) with the physical environment and its social links; the factors explaining their levels of satisfaction were the services provided close by (schools, parks, and so forth).

As against this, the problem area defined and investigated by David Canter (1975) was capable of providing information of more generality and, at the same time, of effecting a deeper analysis of the dynamics of satisfaction. We will use one of his examples because it concerns data already used descriptively; comparison of the two methods is therefore instructive. The survey referred to was carried out by the Building Performance Unit in Scotland and concerned the satisfaction of the teachers with their school, and in particular with their own classroom. Five hundred teachers in 30 different schools answered a questionnaire relating to different aspects of the design of their rooms. The first analysis of these results was in terms of the responses given at a description level for each school. The satisfactions expressed were compared with the architectural characteristics of the schools. Without breaking his data down by school, Canter then investigated the factorial structure of all the individual responses. He obtained three factors: the first was a general satisfaction measure, also including questions about specific physical features such as lighting, heating, view, and room-size; the second factor related to the position of the classroom within the school (central or peripheral); and the third related to the level of satisfaction with the building itself. Clearly, as soon as we have coherent and independent dimensions of satisfaction, it becomes possible to make advances, particularly by investigating the weighting to be given to each dimension so as to produce a priority scale for decisions to be made. It is also possible to correlate each of these dimensions with specific physical aspects of the environment so as to investigate the origin of the satisfaction and annoyances experienced and reported.

The same remarks can be made with regard to the scientific study of nuisance. Let us take the example of noise (Levy-Leboyer et al. 1976). Individuals can be asked to evaluate noise by use of a simple rating scale expressing their annoyance or by answering a multiple-item questionnaire which is analyzed statistically. Two contradictory observations can be made about this type of response. First, the correlation between individual assessments of annoyance and physical measurements of noise is always low. Second, comparing the averages of the annoyance expressed by subjects who are exposed to different levels of noise shows coherent and significant differences. The higher the noise level, the higher the average level of annoyance. This apparent contradiction is explicable in terms of the very great variation in the levels of annoyance expressed. Consensus is weak except in highly exposed locations—yet it is always possible, even when conditions are apparently intolerable and oral communication is impossible, to find respondents who say that they are used to the level of environmental noise. Clearly, in these circumstances, neither protective regulations nor the decisions of planners or builders should be based on crude analysis of expressed annoyance.

It is probable that affirming or denying annoyance caused by noise is a complex judgment. It is therefore necessary to analyze this judgment by means of a series of questions asked together. It is quite possible that a person reporting the presence or absence of noise annoyance is summating four separate opinions. In the first place, he is expressing his attitude toward the very fact of having to express his annoyances and difficulties: in some cultures, this is tolerated, while in others it would be considered a sign of bad upbringing. Second, he is expressing an overall evaluation of the environment in which he lives; for example, if he is satisfied with his house or apartment, he will underestimate the annoyance caused by the noise, and vice versa. Third, the respondent will compare the noise he actually hears with what he expects to hear. Contrary to the hypothesis, residents of noisy apartment blocks who have recently come from a rural area are less often annoyed than otherwise; having decided to move to the town, they accept in advance the idea of exchanging the peace of the country for the distractions and facilities of urban living. In the fourth place, and finally, in making up his mind, the respondent judges the noise according to his personal criteria over a number of dimensions. It is easy to believe, but would need verification by fieldwork, that noise is evaluated from several points of view and that the people who hear it ask themselves if it is useful, if it is dangerous, if it pleases them or seems unpleasant. In addition, they evaluate the annoyance that noise causes them in terms of what they are doing at the time. All of this explains why a general question about annoyance, or a series of responses which are summated without prior analysis, will be a poor reflection of any annoyance that is really due to noise, and will not be sufficient to predict the behavior of the individuals concerned. In evaluating nuisance, it will clearly be necessary to perform factor analyses of the sort Canter used to study classroom satisfaction.

If we really wish to answer the two questions posed above concerning the psychological dimensions of perception and environmental evaluation, then we must have information on a third aspect which has received very little attention so far: the individual's needs with respect to the environment. Are these needs universal or specific to certain groups? What is the nature of the psychological needs which go beyond the most basic (a roof, warmth, physical safety)? Very few researchers have asked themselves this type of question. However, analogous studies in occupational psychology have been carried out over as long a period as twenty years, with interesting results. Current models based on this field work not only give us a list of well-defined needs, but also suggest models of the hierarchical relations between needs and the correlation between satisfaction and the importance of different needs. In addition, work which looks at both differential and social aspects has shown that groups of individuals present hierarchies of specific needs which can be explained by their cultural attachments, occupational experiences, and personal situation.

For this reason, it should be possible to carry out analogous studies to find out what people are looking for in their environment. This is in any case one of the questions most often put to psychologists by architects and planners. It is very tempting to reply to it by carrying out a superficial social survey in which future users of an apartment block or other multioccupied property are asked to pronounce upon their needs. This method does, however, present risks. For example, a survey was carried out among old people, a majority of whom had said that they would like somewhere to sit in the open air, yet sheltered from the wind and the sun. The architect therefore took steps to provide each apartment with a balcony. Nonetheless, the residents were dissatisfied. They did not use the balconies and complained that they reduced the area of their apartments. What they had wanted, in fact, had been a common area in which to sit and chat with others, not a space of their own in which to sit alone. In essence, the need expressed was a social one.

It is therefore very important to go beyond specific surveys which ask specific questions, and to discern the skeleton of psychological needs which underpins the answers given and justifies the choices made. Traditional surveys give "overall" options to respondents which can, however, be motivated by very different needs. Thus, the desire to live outside the great conurbations can represent the need to commune with nature, the desire to be relatively far from neighbors, the wish to have a spacious house, or to live somewhere where one can have control over a large estate. In the same way, wishing to live in a large town can be the result of a need for comfort, or of wanting a lively social life, to be near modes of communication, or even to live near work, which can contribute to occupational success. In short, every "overall choice," whether a response to a question or a decision actually made, represents the result of several needs, and more likely than not the result of balancing costs and benefits.

We can see here the utility there would be in having a precise list of the needs which the environment can satisfy for understanding individual behavior and predicting individual reactions. Kaplan (1973) understood this well and proposed three needs which he thought to be basic. The first is more related to processes within the environment than with the content of the environment: the environment must make sense to those who inhabit it. Next, it must provide novelty, challenge, and uncertainty. To the extent that the unknown becomes known, that the frontier is broken down, the individual is led toward new horizons to explore and master. Lynch's hypothesis comes to mind again: the environment must at the same time be mysterious and coherent. The third need is that the environment must permit choice, that is, the possibility to decide, the freedom to act: change must be offered but not imposed.

This theoretical scheme is very attractive: it has the merit of going beyond the obvious basic needs and relying on more subtle values. It is, however, empirical and therefore needs demonstration. Moreover, it is not obvious that there is a system of universal needs, of the same strength for everybody, no matter what their age, sex, origins, or responsibilities. May the need for uncertainty not be precluded for those who are inherently anxious or those who, because of their family responsibilities, have a stronger need for security?

Because of this gap we carried out a survey of 1500 young French people between 17 and 24 years of age. Factor analysis was applied to the answers they had given to more than 100 questions, based on a large-scale pilot study, and produced seven identifiable and independent needs (Levy-Leboyer, 1977). The first one concerned security and brought together concern for physical security as well as the need for family roots to produce feelings of a firm social base. The second related to the way in which the environment was evaluated. For some, the environment took its value from its intrinsic values—quietude, beauty, integrity, harmony, and so forth. For others, the functional aspects were more important (proximity to work, communications, businesses, and the like). The importance which the environment was deemed to have was a third axis dividing those people who thought the environment less important than the probability of success at work, employment prospects, and salary level from those who, on the other hand, thought the environment important as a means of expression and a sign of social status. Social needs were the object of three distinct concerns: care for integration, as represented by conformity and the possibility of freely choosing one's social contacts; greater or lesser dependence upon the community and its services; and the importance of social life, either based upon the family or externally oriented.

Lastly, a need for participatory activities corresponded to the wish to contribute actively to the planning of the environment, in terms of personal space as well as communal planning. A second survey carried out on older people confirmed the existence of some needs and showed that others disappeared—notably the need for psychological security, which was only weakly felt by married adults, parents, and of relatively high social status (middle class). This group of studies should be considered as a first step which demonstrates a fruitful method. Another approach to this area (Carp and Zadawaski, 1976) used a sample which was both more heterogeneous (2541 respondents over 18 years of age) and more concentrated in interest (all were concerned by a new road system). Factor analysis revealed twenty independent factors which were regrouped into six basic needs by the authors: quiet and the absence of noise, aesthetic environmental quality, neighborhood relationships, security, mobility, and protection against nuisance in general.

The way in which the investigations in this chapter have been developed makes it difficult to synthesize the results concerning environmental perception and evaluation. In fact, it is impossible not to be struck by the existence of major gaps. For example, no investigation has seriously taken into account the role of sociocultural factors as variables in the perception and evaluation of places (although a great many authors report anecdotes or state that there are obvious differences between social groups). Another example is the rarity of field studies of the development of environmental perception, a rarity which is the more striking because of the abundance of laboratory studies of perceptual development. It is also possible to point out the low level of attention given by researchers to the relation between theories of personality and perception. In this case, however, there is the attraction of an exhaustive theoretical model: personality is developed under the influence of environmental experiences and, in addition, it conditions everyday environmental perception and evaluation. Nonetheless, empirical research to test Craik's paradigm or Zavalloni's theoretical model is quite rare. A last example is the way in which, counter to the unanimous position of theorists of environmental psychology, so little attention has been devoted to lifestyle and how its diverse manifestations in everyday life influence the development of perceptions, needs, preferences, and behavior.

Two other difficulties can be seen. On the one hand, it is necessary to use laboratory research as a base, and indeed, every researcher does so, either by alternating laboratory and field work or by reviewing laboratory results before starting out in the field. Nonetheless, it is obvious and well-established that it is the totality of a situation which is perceived or evaluated, with a complex interplay between variables and modulating factors preventing any generalization from the laboratory to the environment. On the other hand, the relative status of verbal and behavioral data is unclear. The differences between them can be stressed but have not been subject to empirical analysis in the field.

Despite all these problems, there are three points which can be discerned as being the subject of total agreement:

(1) The environment is perceived and evaluated as a result of, and by, action. The sequence of behavior is inseparable from the perception of which it is a basic precondition, as one of the sources of feedback, allowing checks to be made that the perceptual process is relevant. More precisely, the perception of the environment depends on behavior in four ways. First, perception is impossible

except in relation to reference data. These reference data, however (especially space, but also the representational devices needed for the process of perception, the structuring of sensory inputs, and for the identification of the external world), are built up in the course of active experience. Second, active exploration increases sensory inputs and allows the essential cognitive activity of detecting invariants to take place. In other words, activity produces a multiplicity of data and a diversity of perspectives, enriching experience and involving the search for stable schemata to order sensory complexity and to interpret external reality coherently. Additionally, as has been amply demonstrated by the Geneva school, behavior demands coordination which becomes finer and finer and more and more adaptive, and which itself demands knowledge of the objects perceived. Therefore, activity stimulates the construction of abstract models. Behavior has a very strong influence upon environmental perception and evaluation in yet another way, linked to what Pailhous (1970) has called the "finalization" of the perceiver: "beyond the constraints of the material world . . . the objectives which the individual sets for himself to achieve are essential for determining . . . the strengths of the object in space." More broadly, research can be carried out on the way in which perception is determined by utility (i.e., by the objectives of the perceiver), whether the perception is for the first time or very frequent. Thus, an Arab guide can perceive paths in the Sahara, an inhabitant of the African forests can identify and use the tracks of an elephant; the gondolier who took Proust across Venice could differentiate canals which seemed identical to the newcomer. Lowrey (1973) has shown empirically that estimations of distances between several points in a town differ according to whether they are made by drivers or nondrivers: drivers make fewer errors in their estimates, but there is less variability among nondrivers.

(2) Environmental perception and evaluation cannot be separated from the temporal dimension. Every perceptual identification, every system of attitudes toward the environment is based upon representations and norms which are acquired by people as a result of individual and cultural experiences. Studies of perceptual development show clearly how systems of mental representations of the environment are built up to allow both the integration of perceptual information and its use as rich and meaningful signs. It is for this reason that the psychological transcends the purely physical, and that the external world takes on a value, or rather a set of values for the perceiver: aesthetic, affective, and so forth. These are related to past experience, direct or indirect. The external world is interpreted as having intentions and po-

tentialities; it is reassuring or threatening. Perception includes an instant prediction of the future, and the environment contains values which are either desired or not desired. To be more exact, past experience plays a triple role in environmental perception and evaluation. In the first place, each individual receives sociocultural norms from his social environment and from the subcultures of the groups to which he belongs or which he joins, and these influence the way in which he reads the world by sorting and deciphering incoming data. In addition, the social environment forms attitudes and specific skills which will determine environmental behaviors—to start by the signals, rules, prohibitions, and recommendations—with which the world seems to be crammed. In the second place, past experience teaches us how to understand the environment in which we live through the constant exchange between perception, behavior, and related feedback. Finally, past experience allows the individual to construct specific expectations of the external world. The confrontation between these expectations and reality is probably a basis for each of us both to evaluate the environment and to take action to make it conform more closely to that which is expected of it.

(3) The third point is both more general and more fundamental. The importance of individual differences is very striking where research into the real environment is concerned. Psychologists of the Freudian persuasion have done a great deal to convince us of the individuality of personal experiences. Even if the relationships between oneself and others or within the self can be analyzed and classified, they are still not less than personal experiences, and the ways in which they are learned and integrated give each individual his individuality. Symmetrically, environmental perception and evaluation can be said to lend themselves to scientific analysis based on concepts and processes which are the same for everybody. Nonetheless, it is certain that the environment which is common to everybody is still particular to each person, since it is perceived through the prism of previous experiences, private valences, and individual activities. If we wish to investigate the determinism of the environment for behavior or individual action in designing the environment, it will be necessary to remember that the environment, as the cause or the seat of behavior, is not the "objective" environment, but is each person's personal environment, perceived, interpreted, and transmuted by the individual personality.

CHAPTER 3

Environmental Stress

Having considered the way in which a person receives information from the external environment and how this is interpreted and evaluated in relation to that person's needs and values, it is reasonable to assess the knowledge we have of the psychological effects of environmental conditions. This type of work, however, is almost exclusively concerned with the negative effects of the environment, which is not at all surprising when account is taken of the applied nature of this research and of the desire to optimize the environment, which has motivated the majority of researchers in this area. The emphasis has been placed on noxious aspects of the environment, with two aims in view: the description of the disturbances caused by unfavorable conditions and the identification of the characteristics which bring about the noxiousness. This chapter, therefore, is exclusively concerned with environmental stressors.

The effects of environmental stress can be studied at a variety of levels. Investigations can be short-term, when we describe the instantaneous reactions to a specific environment (this type of research is often carried out in the laboratory), or longer-term, when longitudinal or comparative field studies are made of populations living in different environments. In addition, the effects which are investigated can be, so to speak, fortuitous and reversible (for example, the effect of noise on learning a particular skill), or can be seen as inherent, as when the environment is considered to be responsible for long-term personality modifications, changes in the social behavior of an individual, or even in social behavior which can be culturally transmitted.

To put some order into this collection of disparate facts, it is important to make some effort at definition. The concept of stress was originated by the biologist Hans Selye in 1936 as a systemic factor: a situation is stressful when an organism reacts to noxious stimulation or is altered by it. There is no question of a dichotomy of reactions between those which are passive and those which are active adaptations, but rather a series of stages in the adaptation process (dubbed by Selye the General Adaptation Syndrome [GAS]) that is observable whenever the organism must face attack or, more generally, face unfavorable environmental conditions. The GAS is characterized by three stages: an alarm period, during which the organism mobilizes its resources; a period of resistance, during which it fights the external disturbances; and a period of exhaustion, during which the fighting capacities of the organism are nonexistent. This last extreme is not always reached, of course, since the ecosystem very often recovers its state of equilibrium. This is just as well, since stress and the organism's reactions to it are not at all exceptional but a part of everyday life. The adaptation, however, is not necessarily benign: the most important characteristic of stress is that it produces biological and psychological activation and these can, by themselves, become sources of serious disturbance (Saegert, 1976).

The term "stress" has now been extended into situations which do not strongly imply physical noxiousness, but in which psychological reactions are the source of tension. In reality, it would seem to be difficult to distinguish, in the case of human beings, between biological and psychological stresses, for a number of reasons. In many stressful situations, biological and psychological causes of stress are present together, and it is therefore very difficult to separate them for research purposes. At one extreme, the question of whether stress can exist without a psychological component can be raised. Mason (1976) has, for instance, exposed subjects to a variety of environmental stresses (extreme heat or cold, prolonged fasting, excessive work), but took care to create experimental conditions which were neither threatening nor demeaning. In this case, the stressful physical variables did not produce the classically observed endocrinological changes. Strictly speaking, psychological research into environmental stress consists, as we shall see later, of the definition of those psychological circumstances which confer a stressful character upon unfavorable physical conditions.

These difficulties made Lazarus and Cohen (1977) criticize definitions of environmental stress which were based entirely upon an inventory of possible causes of stress, and to propose a classification of responses which indicate that a situation is stressing:

(1) Somatic responses, including hormonal indicators, such as levels of catecholamines or corticosteroids, and neuroreticular indicators such as cardiovascular changes, electrodermal resistance, and changes in respiratory rate. It should be noted that these reactions can, by themselves, cause somatic pathologies indirectly related to stress.

(2) Behavioral responses, which can be categorized into three classes: adaptive behavior, which can just as easily be the taking of tranquilizers as actively defending oneself or denying the stress; disorganization of behavior, such as disturbance of skilled performance at tasks, disturbance of information acquisition, "paralysis" due to fear, and so on; and expressive behavior, such as facial expressions and posture changes. It should be noted that adaptive responses can mask this disorganization.

(3) Subjective behavior: verbal expressions, spontaneous or prompted, of experienced discomfort or of the emotional response to stress.

It would be useful to draw up a table of the results of the research to date linking environmental circumstances to specific effects. This is not possible, however, at the present state of knowledge. First, each study only considers one quite specific type of response. Second, the causes of stress investigated in these studies are paired with the usual effects, with the researchers seeking to investigate the traditional hypotheses (the city as a pathogenic environment, density as a source of disturbance of interpersonal behavior, noise as a cause of performance decrement, and so forth). Finally, the "causes" which have been investigated were defined along varying standards of precision.

The size of the city, even the geographical concept of the region, can be the basis of comparison while, at the other end of the scale, studies with extremely narrow aims can be concerned with the behavioral effects of rigorously defined climatic conditions in laboratories where temperature, humidity, and ventilation can be controlled. Under these circumstances, it seems to be logical to start with the most general studies and finish with those concerning isolated variables, thus giving conclusions which are most appropriate for analyzing the processes relevant to adaptation to environmental stress.

THE CITY AS A STRESSFUL ENVIRONMENT

Present-day social scientists are prejudiced against cities, and in particular against large conurbations. However, it would be just as justifiable to contrast the urbanity ("politeness given by worldly experience"—*Littré*) of the city-dweller with the awkwardness of the countryman, and to recall the attractions of the city (its cultural resources, its human richness, the tolerance of the great urban centers) as opposed to the chauvinism of small communities. On the contrary, however, research into urban stress attempts to demonstrate the pathogenic nature of the city. There are two more specific hypotheses which have been put forward: (1) city life is conducive to mental illness and delinquency; and (2) the urban context impoverishes social relations and develops a lack of civility and indifference toward others.

Research into delinquency and pathology has been carried out in a wide variety of countries, and the conclusions drawn seem to be rather similar. In Sweden, Carlestam and Levi (1973) have demonstrated that Stockholm, constituting 16 percent of the total population of Sweden, accounts for 39 percent of all thefts in the country. The type of habitat, just as much as the density, seems to be correlated with criminality. Timms (1971) shows that in Luton, an industrial town near London, 5 percent of the adult population and 3 percent of the adolescent population live in furnished accommodation, while 30 percent of adult crime is committed in those surroundings and 13 percent of juvenile delinquents live in this way. Similarly, Schmitt (1957) reported strong correlations between delinquency and density of population in Honolulu. Interestingly, although he used different measures of density, only two measures (population per acre and the percentage of dwellings in which there was an average of more than 1.5 people per room) were correlated with delinquency. No such relation existed with the size of the family, the proportion of married couples having an independent dwelling, or the number of apartments per building. In Minneapolis and Seattle, Schmitt (1966) reported an association between high population densities and criminality within the center of the city. Delinquency rates were lower outside of town. As early as 1939, Faris and Dunham had shown that mental illness was more common in the "disorganized" zones of the modern city. Other, similar results are given by Michelson (1970) in his book about man and the city. But the conclusions concerning the city and mental illness are less clear. Srole (1972) put forward a number of conclusions in his review of mental pathology in rural and urban regions: (1) as far as children are concerned, slums and shantytowns, whether urban or rural, are equally pathogenic; (2) in the case of adults who wish to change their environment, the city presents a more tolerant setting than enclosed communities, especially for people with deviant behavior. In another survey, Dohrenwend and Dohrenwend (1972) showed a greater number of neuroses and personality disorders in urban areas, but more psychoses in the rural regions.

Although these investigations seem to agree with one another, they do not escape criticism. In the first place, the variables used to represent the environment are too general and badly defined. The constituent factors in pathology are equally imprecise. Indeed, when socioeconomic factors are controlled, the results change in appearance. Winsborough (1965) has shown that the density per acre in the Chicago region was related to infantile mortality, tuberculosis, and use of social services. These relationships, however, disappeared when socioeconomic and educational levels were controlled. In New York, Freedman (n.d.) obtained a correlation of 0.36 between density and delinquency and 0.56 between density and mental illness. Controlling for the average income and percentage of non-

whites, however, removed the effect of density. Freedman concluded that density, whether defined as population per acre or
number of residents per room, was less important than some
had believed it to be. Hollingshead and Redlich (1952) carried
out a finer analysis which showed that the behavior of patients
belonging to the lowest social classes, even though they were
more often subject to mental illness, indicated that they made a
better readjustment to their social group on leaving the hospital
than did those from higher classes. Thus, we should not blindly
accuse the city or its social structure of giving rise to mental
illnesses, although the same factors lead to deprived families
living in deprived environments as to their being more frequently hospitalized for mental illness.

In addition, we must not neglect the impact of cultural differences and must take into account, both for illnesses and delinquency, the behavior which is acquired as a result of crime and
illness. It may be, for example, that there is greater use of institutions in the city, as compared with lower use in the towns and
countryside, both because such use implies a displacement and
because the community is able to put something in its place. To
test this hypothesis, it would be reasonable to compare the expectations held by city residents with those who live in towns of
different sizes regarding social organization and behavior as
against petty crime, pathological symptoms, or cases of devi-
ance. At the time at which this is being written, intercultural
research has shown that there are different methods of adapting
to density in dwellings and obtaining some level of privacy.
Mitchell (1974) suggested that the Chinese accept high levels of
density because they are very reserved emotionally and because
the customs of family life are carefully regulated. David and
Sandra Canter (1971) explained the low level of vandalism, liveliness of urban life, and safety of Tokyo by the fact that the city
is a collection of villages. The Japanese adapt to very high densities by "turning inwards" and also by miniaturizing some aspects of their environment and by drawing aesthetic satisfaction from the perception of detail (as, for instance, in the case of
the miniature bonzai trees). Rogler (1967) showed how norms
relating to respect for the privacy of individuals are developed
in the miserable outskirts of Latin American cities where the

basics of comfort do not exist. Even more clearly, the results of Munroe and Munroe (1972), who made comparisons of African societies living in more or less crowded conditions, showed that the most crowded groups have specific norms for friendship and family relationships which serve to avoid contact with others. In short, the sociospatial conditions of life in conurbations produce modes of interpersonal relationships controlled by rigorous rules which allow people to safeguard the minimum of privacy which they require and to protect themselves against intrusion, despite very high densities.

Finally, even the idea of density itself is imprecise. Zlutnick and Altman (1972) put forward, for this reason, a division of the idea into two aspects: internal density (number of persons per room) and external density (number of persons per unit of urban area). These two parameters are independent of one another and can be used to describe different situations. The two densities are low in residential suburbs and high in city centers. In rural areas, the external density can be very low while the internal is very high. The reverse is true in the luxury areas of large cities. In addition, the proportions of the different conditions can change. The recent multiplication in Paris of high-status tower blocks of apartments along the banks of the Seine has increased the external density of an area which was previously occupied by people of low income, while the internal density has gone down. In the same way, Murray (1977) has put forward a third measure, inspired by ecological considerations: the ratio of population to resources. At the macro-level, this is an economic index. If the site chosen for the calculation of the index is functionally defined, it is an ecological index: the number of people in a bus, a store, or a doctor's waiting room. Finally, other investigators like Hutt and Vaizey (1966) have distinguished between the effects of social density (many people in the same place) and spatial density (little space for each person)—a distinction that opens the way for a study of the psychological processes produced by lack of space. None of the conceptual analyses of density is an intellectual game. On every occasion that a piece of research uses different indices simultaneously, the results can be shown to vary according to the index used (Schmitt, 1966; Chombart de Lauwe, 1959; Gall et al., 1972).

The second group of investigations is concerned much more specifically with the behavior of the city-dweller. These investigations attempted to give an objective meaning to the idea of incivility and to show that this is a consequence of life in the great conurbations. A variety of techniques have been used (Milgram, 1976; Korte and Kerr, 1975; Merrens, 1973; Forbes and Gromoll, 1971; Korte et al., 1975). Generally, the inhabitants of large cities (and especially New York) were shown to be very much less cooperative than those from small towns, in a variety of circumstances; for instance, helping a stranger find the address of a friend whose address has been lost, opening the door and allowing the use of the telephone, giving information over the telephone to someone who has the wrong number, posting a "lost" postcard, telling a stranger that he has dropped a key, speaking to an interviewer in the street, or trying to help a foreigner who is looking at a streetmap. However, although the results are clear when New York is compared with other towns, they become inconsistent when the comparisons are among small and medium-sized towns. Further, similar experiments carried out in the Netherlands failed to show the distinction between the city and the small town in a comparison of Amsterdam, the Hague, and four small towns. In this context, it is possible that the reactions of the New Yorkers relate to concern for their own safety (Korte et al., 1975).

It might be better, rather than looking for styles of behavior which typify all city-dwellers, to look at regional and cultural differences. Two studies can be cited in support of this contention. They do not constitute demonstrations of it, but they do provide indications. Zimbardo (1969) abandoned two cars without number plates and with their hoods open, for periods of 64 hours, one near the Stanford University campus at Palo Alto, California, and the other near the New York University campus in the Bronx. In New York, a family—father, mother, and a son of eight years—removed everything from the glove-box and the trunk, together with the battery and the radiator, all within the first ten minutes. At the end of 26 hours, the car no longer contained anything that could be salvaged. In Palo Alto, however, nobody touched the car except a passerby who closed the hood because it was raining. Feldman (1968) compared the behavior of inhabitants of Athens, Paris, and Boston in five situations: (1) someone asking them the way; (2) a stranger asking a resident to post a letter; (3) a stranger asking a resident if the latter has dropped a dollar bill to see if he will tell a lie; (4) a clerk giving a stranger change if a bill has been overpaid (5) taxi-drivers taking extended routes so as to overcharge strangers. A large number of observations (more than 3000) showed that there were detectable differences in the ways in which strangers were treated in these different cities. People more easily gave directions in Paris and Athens than in Boston. Only the Parisians would post the stranger's letter and resist the temptation to keep the dollar bill. Paris taxi drivers, on the other hand, overcharged foreigners more than other French people, which did not apply to Athens or Boston.

In reality, of course, it has to be asked whether research into such universal variables as national culture or the size of cities has any real chance of explaining the variance in social behavior. The sociological perspective of defining the city generally, in terms of its influence on the differentiation of roles, the dominant technology, and the economic alternatives offered to its inhabitants, and of looking for the consequences which flow from these characteristics, seems to be too brief a summary. Ecological investigation, consisting of defining a city by its attributes (e.g., size, density, heterogeneity), represents another approach, perhaps a more fruitful one. It can have two concrete manifestations: (1) the systematic investigation of samples of respondents from environmentally different sites corresponding to the aims of the study (e.g., city or town); (2) research devoted to characteristics of the urban environment.

The classic example of the use of the first model (in the name of ecological psychology) was that by the team led by Barker and, more specifically, by Wright (1967) to investigate comparatively small and medium-sized communities (average size 600 and 30,000 people, respectively). A construction game was given to children so that their representation of the town could be analyzed. The analysis showed that there was a much larger number of elements in the medium-sized communities and that, despite this, the children living in the small communities had a wider and more differentiated knowledge of their environment.

In order to find out whether these differences were related to the real level of acquisition of the children or to what they wanted to say on the matter, each was interviewed in the course of a walk around an area defined by the 50 houses nearest his/her home. This showed, for example, that the small-town children knew, on the average, the jobs of 20 of the adults who lived near them, compared with an average of 7.5 in the middle-sized towns.

Wright's group went on to investigate whether these differences were in fact a function of differences in the children's experiences. An activity survey was carried out which gave information about the number of places known to the children, the time spent there, and so on. This showed both similarities and differences between the two groups of children. They spent very similar amounts of time in the public parts of the town, but the small-town children revisited the same sites more often and spent about twice as much time there as the children from the middle-sized towns. This difference arises because the larger town has more resources which are used less often and for shorter periods of time. The better knowledge of the environment displayed by the small-town children is probably explained by other factors. For example, they went out more often without an adult escort.

Another member of the group investigated whether children in cities lived within less limited communities, closer to those typical of small towns (Adelberg, 1979; Gump and Adelberg, 1978). The results showed that city children went outside their district more often than the others, whether they lived in a small or middle-sized community. In addition, city children went more often to shopping areas but less often to cultural or social facilities (clubs, sports grounds, and the like), and more often to areas specifically for children but less often to those principally for adults. All the details of these studies are concrete and indicative and lead to two conclusions: studying the lifestyles and cognitions of matched groups living in different environments produces a great deal of useful information; it also allows us to show how environmental conditions determine lifestyle which, in turn, determines the type and nature of environmental cognition. It would probably be possible to develop this methodology and attempt to explore the relative roles of the environment and other social variables (socioeconomic status, family size, and so forth) on lifestyle and cognitions.

Another method of improving on the inexact results with which the descriptions of behavior in different types of town leave us consists, as described above, in looking at each characteristic of urban life separately. In the Dutch study already referred to, the investigators did not observe any differences in civility between the inhabitants of large and small towns: they then went on to describe with greater precision each of the sites at which the data had been collected. In this way they were able to show that a composite of four indices (sound level, density of traffic, pedestrian density, and number of buildings visible) was inversely proportional to the frequency of helping behavior, especially when it was a matter of spontaneous help offered to a stranger with a map in his hand. It is possible, therefore, that it is the number and intensity of stimuli which comprise the stress variable responsible for aggressive and uncivil behavior.

A corpus of work exists concerning those environmental variables which are considered capable of causing stress. These studies are particularly related to sociospatial density and noise. Within the same context, and despite the fact that they are not particular characteristics of towns, investigations have been made of the effects of abnormally high or low temperatures. Since the conclusions from these studies have points in common with those concerned with noise and density, they will receive the same attention in the paragraphs which follow.

SOCIOSPATIAL DENSITY

Research interest in the psychological consequences of density is relatively recent and has been stimulated, without a doubt, by research carried out on animals. Dubos (1965) described impressionistically the periodic migrations and collective drownings of the Norwegian lemming. These migrations are accompanied by metabolic dysfunctions. The same phenomenon of death on a large scale has been observed by Christian et al. (1960) in a herd of deer which had grown to the point of overpopulating a Maryland island. The brutal increase in mortality rate is also related to metabolic disequilibrium and glandular changes, and comes to an end as soon as the density has returned to normal. The laboratory work of Calhoun played a decisive role in showing the ill effects of density on rats. The lack of space and the growth in the number of animals within a limited area produced serious disturbances of sexual and maternal behavior, even if food was distributed in sufficient quantity. Additionally, males affected by excessive density showed a variety of reactions: either they became totally passive and moved about like sleepwalkers, ignoring the other rats, or they became hyperactive and displayed homosexual and cannibal behavior. Calhoun's descriptions appear to be a caricature of the common social deviations of societies with high urban population densities.

It is obviously necessary to be wary of loose analogies. It is as dangerous to interpret human behavior in terms of the results of animal psychology as to do the reverse. In the last ten years, experimental investigations of density as a factor in individual behavior have made progress toward the analysis of conditions of high density and the definition of categories of density encountered in real life.

In particular, Stokols (1972, 1976) has attempted to differentiate crowding and density. Stokols defines density as a strictly physical variable (the number of people per unit area), while crowding represents, in his view, a subjective state: the feeling of being in a situation where there are too many people. This personal evaluation could be due to the smallness of spaces (as in a submarine or spacecraft) or to the presence of a large number of people in the same place, however large that place is. Altman (1975) noted that the feeling of crowding corresponds to qualitatively different situations according to whether space is limited (as in a dormitory), facilities are difficult to get to (a crowd in a shop), there is frequent intrusion into an individual's private space (as with a large family in a small home), or a short exposure time (as in a packed elevator). In the same way, Stokols differentiated between primary environments, in which people spend the greater part of their time and where they indulge in their major activities, and secondary environments, which are transient and anonymous (means of transport, sports grounds, cinemas, stores, and so forth). Density can be a source of stress in all these situations, but it is obvious that the injuriousness of density and the tolerability of crowding are different according to whether we are concerned with lack of space, intrusion, rationing of essential resources, or with primary or secondary environments. On the other hand, low density can also be a cause of dissatisfaction. A reception at which the guests are fewer in number than the hostess had hoped for, or a play performed to a half-empty theatre, is not maximally enjoyable.

In short, density has a subjective aspect, an interpersonal dimension, and consequences which are influenced by the activities of the individual. It is therefore not surprising that experimental results concerned with the effects of density are often contradictory. Investigators examine different aspects of density or, in more extreme cases, laboratory work is concerned with only short-term exposure to density. It is therefore difficult to present a clear review of the research which has been carried out.

As far as field work is concerned, the greater part of the research has examined density as a factor in delinquency and illness. In this type of research, investigators have looked at "external" density (the number of inhabitants per square meter of built-up area) and not the density of occupants per dwelling. We have already examined, for the most part, the results of these studies in the preceding paragraphs about the noxious effects of the city. Elsewhere, they have been the subject of a review by Kirmeyer (1978). Kirmeyer concludes that the results of statistical studies which set out to associate population density with mental illness or delinquency have been contradictory. She attributes the diversity of results to cultural differences which make density more or less tolerable, and also to experimental designs which lead to the comparison of samples varied in socioeconomic distribution, without taking this diversity specifically into account. In any case, the studies which do control for these variables produce no clearer results, probably because the factors other than density which influence delinquency and pathology are numerous and varied.

Other field studies have been concerned with the impact of

excessive density in the dwelling on performance, social behavior, and dissatisfaction. Eoyang (1974) has investigated the effects in university residences of density and the absence of privacy on dissatisfaction among students. In a more recent investigation, Glassman et al. (1978) showed that dissatisfaction was related, not to crude density, but to students' preexisting expectations about living conditions in university residences. In addition, Glassman et al. observed a significant relationship with academic results. Students who had to share with two others rooms intended for only two students had significantly lower marks than those housed under normal conditions.

There are many studies concerned with the effects of density on social behavior, but their results are far from coherent. Ittelson et al. (1971) observed that the behavior of patients who had the use of a private room in a psychiatric hospital was more active and sociable than the behavior of those who shared rooms. Eoyang (1974) noted less cooperation and friendship between students occupying rooms with more people than usual in them. Hutt and Vaizey (1966) observed normal children and autistic and brain-damaged children between 3 and 8 years of age under a variety of conditions. For groups of 6 to 12 in number, the abnormal children became more aggressive as the size of the group increased, while the normal children did not display any aggression until the group was bigger. Further, social contacts were less frequent in the biggest groups for normal children, in medium-size groups for the brain-damaged, and in the smallest groups for the autistic children. Loo (1973), however, observing the same group of six preschool children in different situations, saw more aggression in the boys in the biggest room while the behavior of the girls did not change. Murray (1977) confirmed the differences between results for girls and boys. Children from crowded homes gave greater evidence of aggression at school, but this was clearer for boys than for girls. Similarly, neurotic tendencies, as measured by a personality questionnaire, were greater among boys from crowded homes than among girls for the same conditions. Murray consequently put forward an explanation which clearly reveals that density is not a simple variable. In crowded homes, the boys would have been exposed to a greater number of interpersonal contacts, and there would therefore have been more occasions for conflict with their brothers and sisters. This would have led to more punitive attitudes on the part of parents, thus favoring neuroticism. On the other hand, girls who belonged to larger families would have had more responsibilities in family life, which would have been an equilibrating influence.

The results of laboratory research into the effects of density upon verbal reports of discomfort are not very clear. In general, subjects report their discomfort and the dissatisfaction which that causes, but very rarely report any feelings of anxiety. In Griffitt and Veitch's (1971) experiment, heat was added to density, and the subjects evaluated the situation negatively but without speaking of stress or anxiety. The results of Freedman et al. (1971) and of Sundstrom (1973) were the same. There is really nothing surprising in this, since exposure to high density conditions in the laboratory is too short to give rise to anxiety. In addition, the measurements of anxiety were carried out in general at the end of the experiment, just when the subjects were about to be freed from the stressful conditions. Comparisons of laboratory performance on simple or complex tasks (crossing out letters, group discussion, object identification) in crowded conditions have led to misleading results (Freedman et al., 1971; Rawls et al., 1972). Sherrod (1974), however, has shown that there were effects after experiencing the period of density, especially when the source of stress represented by the density was not controllable. Subjects who had performed previously in conditions of high density not subject to their control performed at a significantly lower level, thus mirroring Glass and Singer's (1972) results on noise.

Several studies have shown that subjects placed in high-density conditions have a tendency to be more aggressive and less cooperative. Freedman et al. (1971) analyzed the impact of density on tasks requiring cooperation between individuals. Male subjects showed themselves to be more competitive and demanding in high-density conditions, while the opposite was true of female subjects. Griffitt and Veitch (1971) showed that sub-

jects in hot and crowded conditions gave more negative evaluations of a person whose attitudes were described to them than
did subjects in more comfortable conditions of temperature and
density.

Rohe and Patterson (1975) varied the amount of competition
for available resources in order to show how aggressive and
retreating behavior can be stimulated by density. They made
comparisons between experimental conditions in which spatial
density and availability of resources (the number of toys given
to children) were controlled. In conditions of little space and few
toys, the children were aggressive and played destructively, but
there was little bad behavior when the space was limited as long
as there were sufficient toys. In short, one can only agree with
Altman (1975) and his refusal to draw any general conclusions
about the psychosocial effects of density. It is certain that environmental conditions characterized by an excess of people in a
limited space demand specific adaptive behavior. The type of
adaptive behavior and its probability of success are, however,
influenced by a great number of factors.

The same differences between laboratory and field results,
and the same difficulty in generalizing from one situation to
another, can be observed in the investigations of the effects of
noise and temperature which we next consider.

THE THERMAL ENVIRONMENT

Three reviews of recent research summarize the effects of
temperature (Pepler, 1963; Provins, 1966; Griffiths, 1975). They
give, in particular, descriptions of the effects of extreme temperatures on performance. Mackworth (1950) had subjects perform
four different tasks: receive a message in Morse code, a visual
vigilance task, coding, and tracking. The first three tasks were
affected by upward and downward deviations of the ambient
temperature, with the optimum at about 28-29°C) (the subjects
were very lightly dressed), and a difference from this level of 5
degrees in either direction produced a significant change in
performance. The results obtained by Poulton and Kerslake
(1965) were more subtle. They studied performance at two simultaneous tasks: monitoring five dials, and detecting a re-

peated letter in sequences of 10 letters. The tasks were less well performed in the coldest conditions (21°C) on the first day. On subsequent days, the best results were obtained at the highest temperatures (45°C). Finally, other investigators have recorded no effects of temperature. Dean and McGlothlen (1975) investigated the performance of ten pilots at two simultaneous tasks (vigilance and tracking) and did not find any significant differences, although temperatures varied between 17°C and 43°C. These contradictions are found in both laboratory results and in field investigations. Holmberg and Wyon (1969) and Ryd and Wyon (1970) observed significant differences in the performance of minimally clothed children of 9 to 11 years of age exposed to temperatures of 20, 27, and 30°C. The educational tests were less well carried out at 27°C than at 20°C, but better at 30°C than at 27°C. In a real school, however, Humphreys (1977) did not observe any relationship between behavior of children, as reported by their teachers, and the classroom temperature.

Two explanations have been given for these contradictory results. The first refers to the variables which connect the subject and the task which he is performing. The research reported above relates performance variations to temperature conditions alone. It is obvious that other factors also influence the quality of the performance and can lead the subject to mobilize his own resources so as to maintain performance at his own best level despite adverse conditions. This is especially the case when task-motivation is high. In addition, when the subject is clearly aware of the variation in high performance, it becomes easier for him to check the quality of his work and possibly to keep it at a constant level despite unfavorable conditions.

Another explanation has been put forward by other writers, in particular by Provins (1966). Arousal, the activation level of the central reticular system, is at its minimum when temperature is comfortable. The general level of arousal is increased as temperature rises above, or falls below, that value. At the same time, the tasks which are performed require different levels of arousal and themselves create arousal. This brings about the differing effects of temperature and, in general, temperature effects performance deleteriously when it creates a level of arousal higher than the task would demand. This hypothesis explains the nonlinear relationship observed by Ryd and Wyon, but does not clarify the interesting finding of Griffiths and Boyce (1971) that subjects carrying out a simple pursuit or classification task were not affected by temperatures between 16° and 27°C. However, when they had to perform the two tasks together, there was a significant temperature effect, with the best performance achieved between 18 and 21°C and the worst at 16 and 24°C, with an improvement at 27°C. This nonlinearity appears to be the rule. If the temperature is slightly uncomfortable, performance goes down, but when it is very uncomfortable, the arousal created by the extra stress improves performance.

Heat does not only have effects on performance; it also influences social behavior. Griffitt (1970) showed that interpersonal relations are more negative and critical at elevated temperatures (more than 32°C, 90°F) than in normal conditions (20°C, 68°F). These results were confirmed by those of Griffitt and Veitch (1971) on the combined effects of crowding and density.

In total, although experiments upon the effects of uncomfortable temperatures are relatively few in number and there is not a great deal of variation in experimental situation, one cannot but be struck by the parallels between the two sources of stress which have just been reviewed. In the two cases, density and temperature, the same variable can constitute either a stress which alters behavior and disturbs performance or a stimulant which improves the results. In both cases, as well, the situational characteristics can have so much influence on the subject-task relationship that the subject can mobilize his resources, adapt himself to uncomfortable conditions, and preserve his level of performance, if he is so motivated. Similar conclusions can be drawn from many studies of the effects of noise.

NOISE AS A SOURCE OF STRESS

Noise has been the subject of considerable interest for a number of years, probably because it is one of the nuisances which modern technology and developments in transportation have increased most noticeably. The early research concentrated on physiological effects, especially on the effects on the auditory apparatus itself, and then on the annoyance felt by people exposed to continuous or impulsive noise, particularly transportation noise (train, road, aircraft) and those transmitted within buildings (noise from household appliances, television or radio, footsteps and voices, and the like). The priority given to subjective reactions is probably explained by the fact that noise has no objective definition. A noise is a sound or a collection of sounds which is unpleasant to the listener and annoys him, either because the noise is physiologically intolerable or because it interferes with other auditory perceptions which are more pleasant or more important. The necessity, for legislative purposes, of defining the physical characteristics which relate to subjective annoyance criteria has stimulated research in this area. Unfortunately, as we saw in the previous chapter, interindividual differences in the degree of annoyance which people express are very large, and research so far has only been able to confirm the existence of the variability and to define the characteristics which explain it—individual traits and the characteristics of the task or activities being carried out during exposure to the noise. In addition, all the investigators who have concerned themselves with this problem have emphasized the lack of fit between subjective annoyance and the effects of noise on behavior (Levy-Leboyer et al., 1976). Nonetheless, it is still necessary to define levels of noise according to the degree of annoyance caused. Researchers have also shown interest in the effects of noise on performance on the one hand, and on social behavior on the other.

One body of research is concerned with the long-term effects of noise, and probably because the researchers have taken a developmental perspective, these investigations have analyzed the consequences of prolonged exposure to noise on perceptual and cognitive learning in young children. The various results obtained in this area seem to be in agreement. A study carried out by Wachs et al. (1971) showed that language acquisition and attentional development were negatively affected by high levels of noise at home. The researchers collected data on the development of 102 children between 7 and 22 months of age. The level of noise at home was the factor most predictive of

developmental level. Unfortunately, however, the research did
not involve an objective measure of the ambient noise level;
instead, the noise was assessed subjectively by the residents.
Similarly, Goldman and Sanders (1969) have shown that schoolchildren living in noisy dwellings failed auditory tests carried
out in a slightly noisy room, while their performance was
clearly better when working in a quiet room. The authors concluded that the fact of living in a constantly noisy environment
reduces the ability to isolate one signal in a collection of auditory signals.

A notable study by Cohen et al. (1973) provided quantitative
information on this point. Fifty-four elementary school pupils,
living at different levels in a 32-story highrise near a busy ex-
pressway, were tested at reading and auditory discrimination
(the Wepman test). The noise levels measured inside the apartments varied between 55 and 66dBA, depending on height
(66dBA on the eighth floor; 55dBA on the 32nd). The correlation
between the floor and noise level was very high (-0.9). The
correlation between the score on the Wepman test and the
height at which the child lived was also a strong one (0.48) when
the sample was limited to children who had been resident for at
least four years. The correlation between the Wepman test and a
test of reading was also significant ($r = 0.53$). The authors concluded that the noise level in the apartment could explain a
large percentage of the variation in auditory discrimination,
which itself also explained a large proportion of the variance in
reading ability: "Prolonged exposure to noise in everyday life
therefore produced durable effects ... It is possible that the
children investigated have learned to filter noise and adapt to a
noisy environment. This adaptation, however, is at the cost of a
loss of verbal and auditory capacity."

A recent piece of research compared the performance of children in a room exposed to train noise with performance in a
quiet classroom on the other side of the same building. The
results were clear and in support of Cohen's findings. Reading
scores were significantly affected by the location of the room
(Bronzaft and McCarthy, 1975). A French study, carried out
with children near Orly airport who were thus exposed to air-

craft noise, analyzed the results of a variety of tests taken at the beginning and end of the year by two comparable groups of preparatory pupils (Sibony, 1979). The above conclusions were confirmed—children working in a school exposed to noise showed less improvement in reading by the end of the year than children working in a sound-insulated school. In addition, the children from the noisy conditions showed themselves to be more restless and unstable in tests requiring attention.

Another group of investigations concerns the immediate effects of noise on given tasks, and attempts to explore the way in which noise disturbs performance. Studies have been carried out both in the field and in the laboratory. Taylor et al. (1965) asked workers on jute looms to wear hearing defenders. These workers did not like the defenders and did not believe that they would improve their work. Nonetheless, the quantity and quality of their work were in fact improved. In another field study, Broadbent and Little (1960) reduced the noise produced by a film-perforating machine by 10dB, producing an apparent increase in the speed of working. However, when the workers were tested later in a room which had not yet received acoustic treatment, the speed increase persisted. This result can be explained as a "Hawthorne effect"; the fact of having participated in an experiment and the intervention in working conditions increase motivation and performance. Nevertheless, the effects of noise on the quality of work are very clear in this research. In fact, in the non-acoustically treated workshops, operator errors and machine breakdowns due to error were five times as frequent as in the treated areas.

It would therefore seem to be the case that noise does not have a negative effect on the speed of working, but that it does have an effect on the quality of work. As a whole, however, results are not so clear. There is a series of quantitative effects on time-estimation, intellectual performance (Tarrière, 1962), immediate memory (Petrescu, 1969), and even on the sense of color (Kittel and Dieroff, 1971). Broadbent (1954, 1957, 1963) has demonstrated that although speed of working is only rarely affected, accuracy is reduced. In simple tasks, such as pressing a button when given lamps are illuminated, there are more errors around noise. In a vigilance task, reaction time is slowed and the signal is missed more often. Similarly, Carpenter (1962) showed that unexpected signals were less often taken into consideration. On the other hand, noise can be advantageous because it can stimulate and cause the individual to "tunnel" attention. In addition, stress due to noise does not summate with other stresses and handicaps, but compensates for them. Subjects who had not slept the night before the experiment performed better in a noisy room than a quiet one (Corcoran, 1962; Wilkinson, 1963). Noise also lessens the decline in performance with age. Davies and Davies (1975) asked young (18 to 31 years) and old (65 to 72 years) subjects to perform a crossing-out task and a paced vigilance task. The effects of noise were visible in all subjects, but the differences were in the opposite direction. The older subjects, who in the quiet condition, had been slower and less accurate than the younger group, worked faster (with no alteration in accuracy) around noise. It would seem to be useful to invoke the concept of arousal to explain these facts. Noise exerts an arousing influence which inhibits the effects of loss of sleep due to age. If, however, the arousal is excessive, performance becomes disorganized and less accurate.

In reality, matters are even more complex, and the concept of arousal alone does not account for all of them. On the one hand, task characteristics also influence the task's sensitivity to noise. Weinstein (1974) has shown that the general quality of proofreading was not altered by noise. This constant level of performance, however, concealed two opposing tendencies: detection of spelling and typographical errors was improved, while detection of grammatical errors went down. The noise concentrated attention on the least demanding aspects of the task. The selection process is not always the same in the distribution of available attention, since motivation can also play a part. When subjects are carrying out two simultaneous tasks, it is the less interesting task, or that which seems to the subject to be the less important, which is most disturbed (Woodhead, 1964; Finkelman and Glass, 1970; Theologus et al., 1974). By the same token, it is possible to manipulate the instructions experimentally so as to determine which task will be interfered with and which will not when the work is carried out around noise (Weinstein, 1974).

In order to assess the cost of adaptation to stressful conditions, one can investigate the effects of noise after the noise has ceased. Glass and Singer (1972) have shown that even when there is no direct effect on behavior during noise, the noise can nevertheless have a hidden effect. Subjects exposed to impulsive noise during the performance of various simple office tasks were later asked to perform more demanding work: proofreading, puzzles, problem-solving with contradictory data, or social situations. Performance during the noise was not affected, but for all the later tasks subjects who had worked in noise showed decreased performance and, in addition, were less obliging when asked to do a favor. Even more interestingly, the investigators were able to show that the hidden effects of noise could be reduced by specific experimental arrangements other than changing the sound level of the noise. The negative effects were reduced whenever the listener had control over what he heard, even if he did not take advantage of this control (for example, he might have a switch to turn off the noise, but did not use it). Similarly, the negative hidden effects were reduced when the noise could be predicted by the subject, either because the sound occurred at regular intervals or because the subject received visual warning. This, of course, explains why the noise of your own typewriter is less annoying than that from the neighboring secretary's, and why people working on a railway line are less annoyed than those passively subjected to train noise. In a workshop, similarly, if you try to reduce annoyance due to the noise of tools by increasing the distance between workers, the annoyance paradoxically increased. If he is too far from his neighbor, the worker does not expect the noise because he has not seen the behavior which will produce it. Finally, the social meaning of the noise reduces its hidden effects: if the hearer thinks that his situation is worse than that of others, and in an unjust way, the subsequent hidden (and disturbing) effects of the noise will be more marked.

Another ill effect of noise concerns changes in social behavior and, more specially, responses made to a request for help. This type of research has been carried out in the laboratory, and consists of observing subjects placed in naturally noisy situations or ones to which noise has been added artificially. The subjects who had been exposed to confused and noncontrollable noise during their work volunteered less often later on to take part in an experiment which involved their being exposed to low-level and pleasant sounds (Sherrod, 1974). Students who had been selected to take part in an experiment were instructed to administer electric shocks to a third person. It was up to them to choose the number and intensity of the shocks. Those exposed to noise inflicted more, and more intense, shocks (Green and O'Neal, 1969; Green and Powers, 1971). Other investigators created a staged situation. For instance, Page (1977) set up a noise source in a university corridor. Just as a student (unaware that he was the subject in an experiment) was passing the noise source, an accomplice, his arms full of books, dropped a set of sheets of paper. Subjects placed in this situation did not help the accomplice to pick up the sheets as often as those who had not been exposed to the noise. Page also used a real-life situation: a building site near a large store. Pneumatic hammers were at work on this site for periods of 25 minutes followed by periods of about the same length of time during which only the traffic noise was audible. In much the same way as before, an accomplice approached a passerby who had been chosen as a subject without his knowledge and, pretending she had not seen him, dropped a parcel she was carrying. Another series of observations at the same place were concerned with more direct requests for help: the accomplice came out of a telephone booth and asked for change for the phone. In both cases, subjects were less cooperative when exposed to noise, and the effect was stronger for female subjects.

Page (1977) put forward five possible interpretations of these observations: (1) there is an information overload due to a surplus of sensory stimulation from the noise, and the subjects filter the information they receive; (2) the noise is distracting, and the subjects less frequently notice the person who needs help; (3) the noise prevents interpersonal communications in the situation of discomfort, and the subject brings the exchange to an end as soon as possible; (4) the noise creates an unpleasant situation which puts the subject into a bad mood; (5) the noise represents a negative stimulus from which people seek to escape as soon as possible. Cohen and Lezak (1977) investigated whether the effects of noise on social behavior were due to loss of attention. They organized a laboratory experiment on the following lines. Subjects had to learn three-letter nonsense syllables in either quiet or noisy conditions. The syllables were projected on a screen, as well as six slides representing different situations (a woman shopping, two men shaking hands, and so forth) which were projected one by one in the middle of the series of syllables. The results indicated that the noise did not affect the learning of the syllables, but that the slides were less well recognized by the subjects who had worked in the noise. Cohen suggested that this focusing of attention on relevant information explains, at least partially, the changes in social behavior observed during exposure to noise.

FACTORS IN STRESS: ENVIRONMENTAL OVERLOAD AND CONTROL OF THE ENVIRONMENT

Any attempt at a synthesis of the facts about environmental stressors would seem bound to fail. The investigations described in this chapter are specific in character and disparate in kind. They were carried out in a wide variety of situations, from the most traditional laboratory experiment to field observation under difficult conditions. Finally, they often contradict one another.

How do these difficulties arise? First of all, it must be remembered just how empirical is the definition of stressful environments. In fact, there is a logical circularity: whatever produces subjective stress (discomfort, annoyance) or objective stress (physiological or psychological disturbance) is stressful. Even if the definition of a phenomenon by its consequences does not raise any objections in principle, in real life it could encounter considerable difficulties. In fact, the same environmental variable is not always stressful and is not the same to all individuals exposed to it. Examples of this are easily found. Population density, as we have seen, can have effects which are favorable, neutral, or unfavorable depending on cultural and social norms, the activities of people exposed to high densities, the means at their disposal for the control of the density, and the length of exposure. The same considerations apply to noise, in which case the effects can be clearly advantageous (higher levels of vigilance or performance) or definitely negative (deterioration in behavior, frustration, aggression). Even worse, there never seem to be linear or proportional relationships between the stressful physical parameters and the intensity of the effects experienced or observed.

However, the fact that these difficulties apply to all the sources of stress which have been investigated has led several researchers to attempt reviews worthy of attention, in that they go beyond the results of specific studies and put forward psychological interpretations. They therefore contribute to the further development of research (Milgram, 1976; Saegert, 1976; Proshansky et al., 1976; Lazarus and Cohen, 1977; Cohen, 1978; Cohen et al., 1979). All of these authors are, to a greater or lesser degree, in agreement about the way in which problems of stress be approached. In one way or another, they emphasize the *relational* character of stress as a psychological state which is not related simply to either the individual or the environment, but to the inadequacy of the relation between, on the one hand, individual needs and resources, and on the other hand, the characteristics of the environment. In addition, they emphasize the importance of the meaning of the situation to the individual. There no longer seem to be simple relationships between the physical characteristics of the environment and the psychological reactions typical of stress. Lazarus and Cohen (1977), for example, describe an investigation by Mason (1976). Apes and human subjects were exposed to different situations characterized by physical stressors (heat or cold, food deprivation, fatigue) and their endocrine responses were investigated. All situations, however, were carefully arranged so that no psychological threat was present.

The sources of stress which had always produced rises in the level of adrenocorticoid hormones in previous experiments did not produce any effect under these circumstances. In other words, separating psychological stress from physiological stress showed the importance of the meaning attached by the subject to his physical condition. It also drew attention to the fact that the individual is neither passive nor impotent in the environment. In almost any circumstances, the individual is pursuing a specific goal which brings about interaction with the physical environment. Because of this, stress represents to each individual a negative influence, the importance of which is related to both the positive value of the goal pursued and the degree to which the stress can prevent the subject from attaining that goal. The subject who is placed in environmental conditions hostile to the accomplishment of his aims is not comparable with iron filings in a magnetic field. He will attempt to adapt to adverse conditions to the best of his ability. Because of these effects, stress can be said to be double-edged. There are at the same time primary, direct effects of stress upon the individual and secondary effects linked to the efforts expended in compensating for the stress and to the psychological cost to the individual of this adaptation. It is clear that the secondary effects can occur *after* exposure to stress, and that the primary and secondary effects can cumulate and become more serious if the stress is experienced over a long period.

These analyses give clear evidence of the complexity of stress and explain the misleading results which have been obtained in attempting to find simple, constant relationships between physical factors and psychological behavior. If any advance is to be made, three characteristics must be present in investigations of environmental stressors. In the first place, emphasis must be given to a systems approach. This means that no simple relationship can exist, permanently, between environmental variables in isolation and behavior. The effects of all stressful parameters are altered by their interaction with other variables. We must therefore carry out studies of interacting systems of variables, and not of single variables, the effects of which are additive. While no systematic inventory of the relevant variables exists at present, it is clear they fall into three categories: the subject's personality and previous environmental experiences;

his activities and present aims; and the sociocultural conditions
and system of values which they create.

Second, it is necessary to integrate the differential perspective into the investigation of environmental systems. It is not
sufficient simply to describe individual differences. We already
know that for a given source of stress, the way in which stress
arises and the levels of adaptation are both extremely variable
between individuals. Some people are much more sensitive than
others because of their personality structure, some even have
temperaments which drive them to seek out stressing situations
and become depressed when they are deprived of them. There
are also societies which reward stressful lifestyles and value the
heroes who triumph over these difficulties. In short, the fact
that sensitivity to environmental stresses is subject to variation
between individuals can be explained by personality descriptions and scales of values. It is possible, however, to go further
than this and ask about the way in which these variables have
their effects. Thus, we can attempt to describe the *transaction
processes* between the individual and the stressful environment.

This double perspective, the systems approach and the transactional investigation of the stress process, has already borne
fruit. A number of different researchers have identified the intervening variables which are common to all environmental
stresses and which can explain the processes by which the man-
environment relationship can bring about stress (Cohen, 1978;
Cohen et al., 1979; Saegert, 1976; Proshansky, 1976). The value
of these models lies quite clearly in the fact that they can just as
easily be used to explain the harmful effects of noise as those of
high temperatures, crowding, absence of basic comforts, or privacy. The first idea is concerned with environmental overload,
and the second with the controllability of the environment, and
thus freedom of choice.

The concept of environmental overload was first mentioned
by the sociologist Simmel who, as early as 1903, put forward the
idea that living in a city was a source of psychological disturbance in the sense that the excess of information forced the
individual to protect himself by filtering out stimuli or avoiding
social contacts. Miller (1964) developed this idea by emphasiz-

ing that stimulus overload forces the creation of adaptive strategies. It was Milgram (1976), however, who described the mechanisms of adaptation most clearly and showed that they operated simultaneously at the cognitive level (selective attention and sorting information) and at the social and affective level (avoidance of interpersonal relations and the reduction of the affective component of these).

Milgram described six adaptive mechanisms: (1) less time is devoted to dealing with each piece of information. Thus, the social contacts of city-dwellers are reduced to a minimum, while in rural districts time is taken to talk and to listen; (2) low-priority information is ignored; only that which is useful is registered; (3) the input load is redistributed so as to reduce the overload (Milgram gives the example of bus drivers who stop selling tickets); (4) a variety of processes are used to block undesired inputs—phone-answering machines or such coldness of expression as to discourage the caller; (5) stimulus intensity is reduced by a series of physical and affective barriers; (6) institutions are created specifically to deal with the social overload (emergency telephone services, social aid systems). The totality of these defensive processes produces three social consequences, all of which have been observed in research already cited:

(1) Reduction of the awareness of social responsibility. The attitude of people constantly subject to overload tends towards complete mistrust of other people in terms of their needs, interests, and requirements, all of which leads to failure to help people in danger or difficulty.
(2) Reduction in courtesy in interpersonal relations. Polite behavior tends to disappear, there are no apologies when people are bumped into, and people stop giving up seats to the elderly.
(3) Anonymity becomes the rule. There is "disindividuation" which makes everyone alone in the crowd, and this, paradoxically, leads to greater tolerance of all sorts of deviation.

Saegert (1976) contributed to the concept of environmental overload by distinguishing a number of aspects of the concept, the consequences of which would be different. The first is the simple intensity or quality of stimulation (as in the case of excessive noise). This is a source of stress to which adaptation is possible and can be fairly rapid, if the person is motivated. It can produce an activating effect which leads to an increase in performance (see, for instance, the studies of thermal comfort and noise referred to above). The second is related to an excess of different types of information, as in overpopulated urban centers, or in the laboratory when subjects are exposed to multiple stimuli or asked to perform several tasks simultaneously.

This latter aspect, an information overload of the person's attentional capacities, is at the center of the model proposed by Cohen (1978). The central thesis is as follows: stressful situations impose an overload of information on individuals, which forces them to reorganize attention. It is this reorganization of attention which must be investigated if we are to understand the nature and variety of individual behavior in stressful situations. Cohen reminds us of three basic postulates:

(1) human beings have limited attentional capacities;
(2) when the demands of the environment exceed this capacity, a hierarchy of priorities is brought into action and attention is focused on the information which is important to the subject;
(3) if environmental stimuli are present which exceed the capabilities of the individual, this initiates an evaluative process which will permit adequate adaptive processes to be activated.

This analysis allows the prediction of the behavioral effects of stimulus overload upon adaptive capabilities and the way in which they vary according to conditions and context.

An experimental subject who is required to carry out two laboratory tasks at the same time and who is exposed to nonrelevant acoustic stimuli will (as we have seen above) reduce the attention he devotes to the less important task. The same is true if the speed of the task is increased. The same phenomenon can be observed outside the laboratory. When a driver has more demands placed on him by the driving itself, he no longer "hears" the conversation of his passengers or other sounds which are presented to him (Brown and Poulton, 1961; Lecret and Pottier, 1971). In the same way, high population density, causing an increase in the amount of information, also causes tunnelling of attention. Saegert (1976) had people visit the shoe department of a large store, in both busy and quiet periods. The subjects had to describe twelve shoes which were displayed, and after their observation they were asked to draw a map of the department. The accuracy of these maps was clearly lower when the department was crowded.

This reorganization of attention does not only have effects on performance and memory, but also on social behavior. Indifference or aggression towards other people, such as has been observed in people exposed to noise, high temperatures, or crowded conditions in many experiments, can be explained, in Cohen's view, by three possible processes: (1) the information coming from the other person which indicates the need for help is not perceived; (2) the information is received but the receiver does not have sufficient spare attentional capacity to evaluate its significance; (3) the effort which would be necessary to aid the other person exceeds the reactive capacities of the subject mobilized by the other aspects of the situation which are more important to him.

We can be certain that environmental overload explains at least some part of the phenomena observed in stress situations and also takes account of the individual variability in reaction, since the sorting of the large number of pieces of information is a constituent of the process, and this sorting is carried out according to a hierarchy of values and priorities which is characteristic of the person and his aims at that time. A second variable, the freedom/ability to control the environment, allows us to complete the picture, to explain another group of facts, and to extract a single parameter which explains ("historically," i.e., by taking into account the past experiences of the individual) the variation in what is observed.

The original idea comes from Glass and Singer (1972) and Glass et al. (1973, 1977) and concerns the noncontrollability of experimental events. We have seen above that their research emphasized after-effects from noise exposure. At the same time, they clearly showed that these hidden effects are closely dependent on the degree of control over the disturbing noise which the subject has. This control can be perceptual or active; that is, the ill effects of the noise are reduced if the subject can turn it off, even if he does not do so, or if the noise is predictable, either in the sense of being regular or of being announced by a visual signal. In the case of the latter, according to the investigators, the stress is reduced because adaptation to the noise is facilitated by the fact that it is predictable.

Others have confirmed this effect for complex and multiple tasks (Plutchik, 1959; Eschenbrenner, 1971; Sherrod, 1974). Wachs indicated that the effect of noise on children was stronger when they were not able to leave a noisy room. Graeven (1975) showed that subjective annoyance was less apparent for subjects with access to a way of controlling the noise. The same consideration can be applied to crowding, according to a recent review by Rapoport (1975), and to Freedman's recent work, already referred to here. In this case, however, the control is applied in another way. When the situation implies that high density is "normal," meaning that it conforms with the expectations of the individual, there are cultural norms which allow us to predict how other people will behave. The situational control comes both from the existence of known processes of adaptation (see the Canters' work on Japan) and from a given individual's ability to predict the behavior of others. Another method of showing the effects of controllability is to compare the results of laboratory and field work. It is difficult to show the deleterious effects of crowding on performance in the laboratory. It is clear in these cases, however, that subjects know that the period of exposure to the crowded conditions is limited.

The stressful effect of noncontrollability is not limited to noise and crowding. Glass et al. (1977) showed in a variety of conditions (where the stress source could be, for example, an electric shock, frustration in an office situation, or arbitrary discrimination) the roles, as mediating variables, that predictability and controllability could have. They concluded that the negative effects of stress were a function of the unpredictability of noxious stimulation and of the feeling of having little control over the presence of the stimulus.

Thus, it is not always the stimulus itself that is stressful, but the impossibility of predicting and controlling it, since the capacities for adaptation are clearly very large. However, the problem remains of how this incapacity is perceived and whether the situation becomes more stressful in relation to the degree to which the subject attributes the incapacity to characteristics of the environment or to his own incompetence.

Recent work (Klein et al., 1976) has shown that motivation changes when failure affects self-esteem, but remains unchanged when the experimental conditions make the subject blame the environment for the failure. The discouragement which follows the experience of being incapable of controlling one's environment has been the subject of a collection of recent work which it is necessary to analyze as complementing the theoretical models of Cohen, Glass, and Singer. These studies are concerned with the notion of helplessness, which is a depressive state in the long-term, and follows exposure to uncontrollable situations or to random or contradictory reinforcement (Seligman, 1975). Once again, the original research was carried out on animals. A dog which had been given electric shocks against which it could not protect itself could no longer learn adaptive behavior in a situation in which it could escape the shocks, although dogs not previously subjected to this helplessness experience could learn the avoidance behavior reasonably easily. This state of powerlessness can also be induced in human beings (Hiroto and Seligman, 1975; Miller and Seligman, 1973). Subjects experiencing noxious stimulation (noises, electric shocks) or confronted with insoluble problems acquired a feeling of helplessness and eventually became incapable of learning how to control those stimuli which were under their control or else obtained only very mediocre results in problems which were perfectly soluble. Glass and Singer showed, as seen above, that noncontrollability of noxious stimuli produced disorganization of behavior immediately after the cessation of the stimuli. Seligman (1975) suggested that exposure to environments which a man is powerless to control produces a change of attitude in him such that he systematically gives up in other situations where he has control.

Studies of individual differences have been carried out in this area. Krantz et al. (1974), noting the similarity between depressive symptoms and helplessness, suggested that helplessness could, as a contributor to depression, be one of the causes of coronary illnesses. In fact, there is a behavioral style defined as typical of individuals exposed to risk of coronary illness (Rosenman et al., 1966) called Type A behavior. This style typifies those individuals who are exaggeratedly concerned with how their time is used and with exactness in their work, are ambitious and preoccupied with their careers, and who drive too quickly. In other words, they are people who constantly strive not to lose control of their environment. It is possible, therefore, that Type A people are more sensitive than others to situations in which they are incapable of predicting or controlling environmental stimuli when, for example, they experience traffic jams, acoustic environments which they cannot modify, or population densities which hinder their plans and activities.

These models seem to explain satisfactorily the experimental data we have, and the mediating variables which are proposed to explain the stressful effects which some environments have on people do seem to be relevant. Nonetheless, they make us aware of a gap. It is not enough to consider man when subject to stress as acting, motivated, led by plans and intentions. There is a third dimension which Proshansky et al. (1976) recall when they are describing the major need of man in his environment: the maximization of freedom of choice. Each individual is constantly pursuing general or specific goals, long- or short-term. In order to attain these, a man must have unlimited control over his capacities, and especially his vigilance—the possibility of isolating himself or approaching other people as he wishes— and over physical environmental conditions which are consistent with his aims. When the environment is an obstacle to the pursuit of his objectives, he makes efforts to adapt to the situation thus created while continuing to seek his chosen goals and to maintain his level of performance. This adaptation is not, however, without its costs. If he fails, this brings consequences both in the short-term (disturbance of social behavior, irritation, frustration) and the long-term (a reduction in self-esteem which will paralyze further motivation to adapt). If he succeeds, it is at the price of efforts to redistribute attention and rearrange behavior (the social behavior of the city-dweller is an example of this) which will create a new source of disturbance. In other words, when the man-environment system is incompatible with the individual's values and aims, this disequilibrium entails an effort devoted to adaptation which is itself the cause of stress.

CHAPTER 4

Space: The Social Dimension

The analysis and explanation of human behavior in the environment without reference to social organization in all its aspects would be a task doomed to failure. In the same way, only a very impoverished picture of social behavior would be obtained if it were to be forgotten that this involves the use of space. In fact, direct observation allows us to determine how the arrangement of the environment reflects social organization (cultural values, hierarchical relationships, conflict, the nature, quality, and function of groups, and so on). In addition, social behavior almost always takes place in public spaces where each individual defines and defends his own territory. In the factory, the office, recreation areas, business places, in transit, and in school, the space is public and people have to appropriate some of it for themselves, defend this temporary territory, and then relinquish it when their object has been attained. There are in this way constant interactions between individual plans, interpersonal relations, and links between people and their space; it is therefore possible to talk of sociospatial behavior.

In the real world, the area covered by this term is very extensive, and research has developed simultaneously in three different directions, following avenues opened up by investigators with specific interests. The first stimulus comes from animal psychology. Ethologists and psychologists have investigated the manifestations of territoriality, the marking of space, and defense against intrusion. The topic was then taken up by environmental psychologists who had it in mind to generalize to humans the conclusions of animal psychology and who investigated, both within the laboratory and outside of it, the functions of territoriality and the relation of hierarchical status in the group to the appropriation of territory.

A second field was opened up by the work of Robert Sommer on the social and spatial behavior of people living or working in shared spaces. The users of libraries, hospital patients, retirement home residents, people in waiting rooms, diners in restaurants, and those attending a course of lectures all choose the place in which they wish to sit and seek to keep it while it is useful to them, within a variety of situational constraints. Sommer and those who have followed him have attempted to describe the way in which the spatial system is socially regulated and to identify the psychological and situational factors which can explain the diversity of behavior that is observed.

A third direction to the research was given by Hall's book on space as "the hidden dimension." While the two research approaches described above were concerned with shared spaces and the way in which they were used, Hall was specifically interested in the distance between individuals and the way in which that distance is determined by situation, culture, personality, and other social, psychological, or environmental factors. Interindividual space was studied as a modulator of social relations. Hall coined the word "proxemics" to describe this sociospatial variable, and he used the term "personal space" to characterize that space, peripheral to the body, which the individual considers as belonging to him.

There have been several recent reviews of this whole field. The first of these was Altman's excellent summary, *Environment and Social Behavior,* which appeared in 1975; more recently, Altman contributed a chapter to an edited volume published in 1977, which reviewed Hall's hypotheses and the results of the research which they had inspired. There has also been a review in French (Lecuyer, 1976) which showed, among other things, the rarity of such studies in France. We will now describe in order the work on territoriality, behavior in public places, and third, interpersonal distance. Since all of these are concerned with the same basic problem—the control of socio-spatial behavior and the way in which space is used in social relations—we will attempt by way of conclusion to discern the trends which emerge in common from these three different directions.

TERRITORIALITY

There is no doubt at all that research in comparative psychology has made a great contribution to the development of present-day interest in the concept of territory in human psychology. This is quite specifically due to the attention drawn to the social functions of spatial behavior. Hediger (1962) and Ardrey (1966) emphasized the essential role of territoriality in the survival of the species and the group, since territory is a guarantee of safety and therefore of survival, and is also a means of controlling food resources and of affirming the identity of an individual and his species membership. A great deal of data exists to support this position. When personal territory is threatened, especially by intrusion from a member of the same species, passive and active defense behaviors are developed. Lorenz (1969) drew a clear distinction between these aggressive behaviors and hunting activities in which the predator attacks other species. In the case of the defense of individual or family territory, we are really talking about phenomena related to the social regulation of the distribution of shared space.

The concept of territoriality introduced by animal psychology has thus contributed to the development among environmental psychologists of the idea that interpersonal relations are not limited to verbal exchanges, and that the possession of space and also its defense represent an important modality of social exchange. It would, however, be dangerous to push the analogy too far by generalizing from observations of animal behavior to the human situation. As Lecuyer (1976) noted, it is no more defensible to explain human behavior in terms of animal behavior than to do the reverse. He drew our attention, critically, to an example of the analogies which have been made in the work of Lorenz (1969: 282), in which it was argued that "human social organization closely resembles that of rats which, inside their tribes, are peaceful and sociable animals, but that behave like veritable demons towards members of the same species but of different communities.

Altman (1975), Ittelson (1973), and Canter (1975) have all criticized the assumption that territoriality is similar in animals and man, for the following reasons: First, aggressive defense of territory is instinctive in animals. Without being dogmatic, the same cannot be said for man, for whom it is the result of voluntary actions, bringing into play the concept of property. In addition, it is obvious that social relations in man are played on more numerous and subtle keys, because of written and spoken language. Settling territorial disputes, in particular, can involve amicable or legal negotiations. Furthermore, animal territories are limited to the space which the animal can control directly. This is not the case for man: on the one hand, each person belongs to a number of social groups with which he shares a series of territories; on the other hand, he also possesses cognitive territories (cultural heritage, patents, copyrights, and the like) which are of importance. There are also different degrees of territoriality from the familial home up to the geographical area that makes up his country, via district, town, and region. On the whole, if one wishes to compare the functional aspects of territoriality in man and animals, then for animals it revolves around biological functions linked by ethologists to the survival of the species, while for man the functions of territory are more diverse and complex.

The comparison between animal and human territory brings out the complexity of this idea when it is applied to man. It is to be expected, therefore, that the behaviors intended to mark the ownership of territory and the reactions to intrusions into the owned territory will be both more numerous and under more complex control. Several writers have tried to classify territories according to the ways in which they are used. The clearest classification is that of Altman (1975), who attempted to take into account at the same time both the degree of control exercised over the territory by its occupants and the duration (long- or short-term) of the possession of the territory by the same user. He distinguished three types of territory: *primary* territory is possessed permanently by groups, and violation by intrusion into the territory represents an affront to and an attack on the identity of the occupant. Thus, in a hospital, the doctor's office and nurses' room are forbidden to patients; or in a school, the teachers' common room is reserved for the teaching staff. *Secondary* territories are divided into a number of subcategories. They are essentially areas over which certain individuals or groups have power or control but where others nonetheless have access. By way of example, Lyman and Scott (1965) drew a distinction between "home-territories" (bars where regulars meet, districts selected by specific ethnic groups, open spaces taken over by a group of children) and territories for interaction, where social meetings of all kinds can take place spontaneously (e.g., the public rooms of hotels or universities). These territories can also be group territories, such as are found, for example, in warships where particular spaces are reserved for the work and leisure of particular occupational groups and to which others have access only at certain times and under certain conditions. *Public* territories are only occupied for short periods and in an unstable manner, and access is relatively free even if there are rules which differ according to time of day, as in public parks, museums, beaches, and playgrounds.

Investigators have shown interest in how public territories are "marked," especially when a person wishes to indicate that his space is reserved and to defend it against intrusion while he is away for a time. A variety of observations (Sommer and Becker, 1969; Becker, 1973) carried out in libraries, restaurants, student residences, and near drinks dispensers have shown the effect of the simple presence of a person near the machine or the empty table. Marking the place with a personal possession (a jacket or an exercise book) was more effective than merely leaving a library book there, and the more objects left to reserve a seat or a table, the more efficient was the control. As Altman has noted, the sole significance of these markers is that the possession of a fragment of shared space can be indicated with objects which are symbolic. The same is true of studies of the efficiency and significance of the hedges, walls, or fences which mark the frontiers of a private garden.

Reaction to the invasion of territory obviously varies according to the category of the territory and will obviously be stronger for primary territory than for secondary, especially for space reserved for a short time in a public place. Several writers have also attempted to classify reactions. Lyman and Scott (1965) distinguished between *violation,* the illegitimate use of a shared but restricted territory (as in the case of the second-class passenger who goes into the first-class waiting-room), and *invasion,* when an individual enters a space which is forbidden him (for example, when a customer in a department store walks behind the counter to serve himself from the shelves). Goffman (1971) proposed other, more subtle transgressions: *obtrusion,* where the person takes up more space than is normal (a man and his parcels taking up two seats in a crowded subway car); and *contamination,* in which a person makes a shared space unclean by spitting or urinating in it. All of these types of intrusion in a space which does not belong to the person, or in which he does not behave according to accepted norms produce, with respect to strangers, protective and defensive reactions in individuals or groups who believe themselves to have rights over the territory or over the manner in which it is used. These reactions are shown in a variety of ways, from the use of language, through an implicit attitude of exclusion (e.g., the indifference of the staff to someone who enters a bar where he is not one of the regulars), to physical violence.

It is not only the nature of the territory and its openness which determine the vigor of defensive reactions to an intruder. The strength of group or individual attachment to the territory is also an important influence. In other words, we need to take account of the totality of the situation in order to understand how an intrusion comes to be considered serious or inoffensive. Researchers who have attempted to show aggressive appropriation and defensive behaviors have been limited by working in those confined environments in which the area available is limited and space is a definitive means of access to local resources (entertainment, food, and so forth). For example, Esser (1970) observed a group of 22 psychiatric patients for 16 weeks. He showed that there were status inequalities, and that the power hierarchy was indicated by a greater or lesser degree of control over the shared space. One third of the group were able, in fact, to go anywhere they wished; another only had access to defined territory for social contacts; and the last were in the most disadvantaged category, since they were only able to use very restricted spaces which were inconvenient for contacting other people. There is, therefore, a social language for space, and this despite the fact that the subjects of that investigation were schizophrenics whose verbal and social interactions were practically nonexistent.

Lipman (1967) also made observations within a confined environment, an old people's home, and emphasized how vigorous were many of the appropriation behaviors. The chairs in the common room were each associated with a particular occupant. This possession had an affective value so strong that people who were displaced from the chair to which they felt entitled went as far as to hit the intruder. Altman and Haythorn (1967) created restricted living spaces in the laboratory and investigated the behavior of subjects who were isolated for shorter or longer periods. They observed that the development of territoriality and the appropriation of ordinary objects (chairs, crockery and cutlery) were a function of the social relations between the subjects. If the subjects were incompatible, i.e., both typified by strong needs for dominance, territoriality and appropriation developed more rapidly.

In yet another study (Altman et al., 1971), the same investigators compared the behavior of subjects who completed the whole isolation experiment (eight days) with that of those who gave up before the end. Those who completed the experiment displayed marked territorial behaviors from the beginning, but in the subjects who gave up, these behaviors only developed slowly. Defining territories and the ownership of objects therefore represent an efficient adaptive mechanism in conditions which are stressful because of isolation or confinement. This value, which the social regulation of territorial behavior has, can also be observed in ordinary life. Altman et al. (1972) brought to our attention the fact that in an apartment or house shared by different members of the same family, there are clearly defined territories: everyone has a place at table, father has his armchair in the lounge, each child a drawer for toys, and so on. These appropriations make life easier and evolve in relation to needs. The small child's bedroom belongs as much to the mother as to her son; as he grows up, he will arrange it in his way and take it over progressively, and by the time he is a young adult his mother will not enter it without knocking on the door.

The sociospatial behavior of human beings in common territory can therefore be said to have two main functions: to reconcile the simultaneous pursuit of different objectives motivating the members of the group assembled in the same place, and to leave each member of the community free to develop his social identity by means of the objects and spaces which belong to him. Although these conclusions seem justified in a general way, the differential psychology of territoriality remains to be elaborated. It is certainly possible to show how dominance relations can determine the territory which is controlled. Other research shows this sort of effect. For example, Long (1970, 1971, 1973) observed the territorial behavior of a college class for a period of 16 weeks. He showed that there was a positive relationship between leadership ability in pairs, and territorial dominance. Over the course of weeks, however, the situation changed socially as cliques formed, each with a leader and a territory. It was inside these subterritories that dominance had its spatial consequences.

Sundstrom and Altman (1974) observed, in the same way, the spatial behavior of young boys in a rehabilitation center. They also observed the relation between the territory controlled and individual prestige. When the social structure of the group changed suddenly, however, because of the departure of two very dominant subjects, there was no longer any evident relationship between territoriality and prestige.

In short, dominance produces the control of territories which are bigger and more valued but strictly within the group, and this relationship only occurs when the social structure of the group is stable. Furthermore, none of these studies take into account one essential element, which is the strength of the need experienced by each individual for the ownership of territory, or even of personal objects. In the study already described in Chapter 2 (Levy-Leboyer, 1977), the majority of the young people questioned anonymously said that it was unpleasant to have a stranger use their things, while 25 percent were indifferent to this or did not find it disagreeable. A communal society in which everything belonged to everybody was judged to be practical by 47 percent of these young people. Clearly, we need to know which subjects are attached to "their" territories and "their" things, what the psychological basis for this attachment is, and who the people are who can tolerate, or indeed wish to have no ownership, even of personal objects.

THE ALLOCATION OF SHARED SPACE

Very frequently, a group of individuals of varying status will come together in one place for a very specific purpose (e.g., a trial, a course, an administrative hearing). Detailed and accepted rules control the way in which each individual chooses his place when we are concerned with a well-defined social event. This is the way in which rules of etiquette indicate the correct places at a table for a meal or for a meeting attended by officials or representatives of countries or organizations. Proximity to the chairman of the meeting or the master of the house has an obvious symbolic value, as does the quality of the chair (for example, a throne, often elevated and ornamented, represents power and authority). The judicial system also follows precise rules about the relative positions of judges, jury, witnesses, the accused, the press, and the spectators. There do, however, exist situations where the individual has much greater freedom to choose his seat. How does he do it? Which characteristics of the subject and the situation explain the differences in the choice?

Sommer (1969) tried to answer these questions by asking subjects to indicate, on a drawing of a table with six places, the seat which they would choose and where they would wish their partner to be, with different purposes in view. For talking, the subjects placed themselves in the corner or face-to-face; to work separately, diagonally or face-to-face; for working together it was most often side-by-side (51 percent), but also face-to-face or in the corner. These results were confirmed by field observation. In a library, places are successively occupied according to a reliable plan (first of all, one reader at each table, and then, when all the tables are taken, second occupants join diagonally from the first; i.e., as far away as possible). When pairs of subjects were asked to discuss a topic and were offered parallel pairs of sofas, they sat face-to-face if the two sofas were not more than three feet apart, and side-by-side if the distance was greater. The same observation has been made of the use of two pairs of armchairs. Social intention therefore has a strong influence upon the choice of seat. Steinzor (1950) had already noted this for leaders, who always try to secure the position at the end of the table, from which it is easier to dominate.

When a whole group enters a room, the choice of the members of the group is relatively stable. Subjects introduced into a square room with a number of unoccupied chairs and who are then asked to sit down and read chose preferentially those seats which face the door (Moore and Feller, 1971). Where the speaker is situated is also an important element. Canter (1969) had eight students enter a large room in which they were to have a seminar. If the seats were arranged in parallel lines, the students took up seats in the front rows if the lecturer was reasonably far from the audience, and at the back if he was closer. For seats arranged in arcs of a circle, the distance of the speaker had no influence. In addition, Batchelor and Goethals (1972) have shown that a circular arrangement is spontaneously chosen by students. These researchers had students enter a room in which the chairs were stacked in a corner. If the group had to carry out a joint case-study, they spontaneously adopted the circular arrangement, which facilitates communication.

In short, the aims which people have when they position themselves, as well as the fixed elements in the environment, determine the behavior of the subjects, since they seek to use places so as to best attain their objectives, be it working alone, conversing, hearing others, or whatever. In reality, as some research (unfortunately not enough) has shown, previous social experiences also influence this choice. Lecuyer (1974) used a particular stratagem. In the first part of his experiment, a group of four subjects and the experimenter were in discussion at a round table, and after twenty minutes an accomplice entered and told the group to leave the room. This was accepted by the experimenter, and the accomplice showed them another, unoccupied room with a rectangular table and five chairs, which the experimenter entered after the group. It was observed that the subjects who had been near the experimenter in the first part of the experiment, and thus had played an important part in discussion, placed themselves at the end of the table, taking advantage of their social position. The subjects changed the spatial arrangement, but did so in order to maintain the previous social structure.

Over a longer time scale, the influence of sociospatial experience is also clear. Baum and Valins (1977) compared the behavior of two groups of students in a whole series of experimental situations. They all lived in university residences, which could be of two types. In the "corridor" type, the rooms were arranged along a corridor, at one end of which was a common room and at the other a very large bathroom. In the "suite" type, four rooms were grouped around a small sitting room and a little bathroom. The average space per individual was much the same in the two cases, but the shared rooms were used by a much larger group in the case of the "corridor" type than in the "suite." Therefore, the students in the corridor block had a much stronger impression that they lived in a crowded environment and said that they tried as far as possible to avoid contacts with the others and looked for means of isolating themselves.

In the first experiment, two groups of subjects, one from each type of residence, were brought together on the pretext of an experiment on psychomotor performance and put in a waiting room where there was already an accomplice. They were observed for five minutes by means of a one-way mirror. It was apparent that the students from the corridor residence sat systematically further from the accomplice, had less verbal interaction with him, and looked at him less often than the students from the suite residence. In an empty waiting room, however, the behavior of the two groups was similar.

The second experiment, with the same two groups of subjects, looked at Schachter's (1959) well-known hypothesis, according to which the company of others relieves anxiety. This time the experiment took place in a dental surgery office. They were told that they would receive electric stimulation of the teeth and gums and had to indicate when they perceived the stimulus and also the pain threshold. Having been thus informed, they were led into a waiting room in which there was already an accomplice. In an analogous situation, Schachter had observed that the subjects, made anxious by the procedure, sought the company of others, especially of those who would be exposed to the same experiment—being more likely to seek others, the stronger their anxiety. Schachter's results were repeated for the subjects from the suite residence, but not for the others, who placed themselves away from the accomplice in the waiting room and did not attempt conversation with him. In addition, when, at the end of the experiment, subjects were asked if the presence of another person had been a comfort to them, only suite residents responded positively.

In sum, without going so far as to speak of a "sociospatial personality," it does seem obvious that the way in which an individual positions himself in a shared space depends upon social and psychological factors. In particular, these behaviors follow from the aims of the individual and the way in which his distance from others is integrated with his plans. They are also a function of the social status of the individual in the group which is occupying the space and the situation or the event which is taking place. Finally, the behavior of each person is influenced by his previous sociospatial experiences, even if he is not capable of perceiving them clearly or of making explicit the attitudes which he acquired from earlier experience. Thus, there is no sharply situational determination of spatial behavior nor a uniquely individual one, but rather a transactional relation linked to the meaning of each situation for each individual and to earlier experience. The same types of problem have been raised in studies of personal space, which are about to be described.

PERSONAL SPACE

The first descriptions of "personal space" were made by Hall (1966). He called the field of research which was concerned with the diversity of these spaces and the factors determining their size and function "proxemics." As before, we are dealing with behavior which is both social and environmental, since the question posed is essentially this: What degree of proximity to others will people tolerate in different situations? Some writers go further and define personal space as an invisible bubble surrounding the body of each of us and to which strangers do not have access. This territory would in some way be carried about by us and considered as belonging to us. Such space has an affective significance and is protected when there is intrusion. The size of the bubble can be investigated in relation to defensive reactions in terms of cultural, individual, and situational differences. Hall's hypotheses have inspired a great deal of research, systematically reviewed recently by Altman and Vinsel (1977). Elsewhere, the definition itself of personal space has been criticized at the conceptual level. It would therefore seem to be useful to start by summarizing Hall's ideas, his typology of personal spaces, and his hypotheses about their origin, then to identify the criticisms which have been made of the basic idea, and finally to examine the experimental evidence, with the help of Altman and Vinsel.

Hall distinguished four spatial zones which serve to regulate our different social interactions: intimate distance, personal distance, social distance, and public distance. *Intimate distance* includes a near zone (0 to 15 cm) and a further zone (15 to 45 cm). At this distance you can receive from the other not only visual information, but also auditory and olfactory, and even touch and temperature. In public, this proximity is not considered to be suitable. If we are forced into this situation (for example, on a crowded subway), we react by assuming a lack of expression, an upright stance, looking in another direction, and avoiding touching other people. *Personal distance* is between 45 and 75 cm for the near space and 75 and 125 cm for the farther zone. This is the protective zone which everybody maintains between himself and others. Interpersonal communications are still rich, because two people can still touch by holding out their arms, some odors are perceptible, and visual details and sounds are still numerous. This is the distance used in public for normal contacts.

Social distance extends from 1.25m to 2m for the near zone and from 2m to 3.5m for the farther one. This is still a distance which allows communication. For example, this is the distance between two people speaking in an office or two colleagues working in the same room. It does not allow any touching, but facial expressions and posture are easily visible and conversations can take place in a normal voice. It is therefore the distance which is used for public and professional relations where social contact is necessary but where there is no implication of friendship.

Public distance goes beyond 3.5m (near zone 3.5 to 7.25m, farther zone, more than 7.25m). It is a formal distance which, for example, usually separates a lecturer from his audience, or the opposite sides in a negotiating committee. This distance still allows visual observation of posture and expression, but forces people to adopt a more formal and better articulated tone of voice.

Hall's fundamental idea is that the different criteria which define the relations between distance and social situation are not universal. The numerical indications given above would correspond to the behavior of Americans and could be subject to great variation as a function of culture, circumstances, and personality. This hypothesis has formed the basis of many pieces of research, which is in fact very desirable since Hall himself gave only examples of cultural differences. According to him, Germans defend themselves particularly vigorously against intrusion into their personal space, the French like closer contacts and visual communications, and Arabs, in general, tolerate shorter interpersonal distances than Westerners.

A variety of authors have criticized the very idea of personal space using basically similar arguments. Lecuyer (1976) emphasizes the social dimension of space and therefore argues that "personal" space is the wrong term. This is not a purely formal remark, since it is dangerous to interpret the personal space dimension or reactions to intrusion without taking account of the nature of each situation. It is the interpersonal distance compatible with a given mode of communication which is observed in each real situation. This clarification is important theoretically, because we should not be talking about a personal space, individual to each person and resulting either from instinct or cultural conditioning and carried about by each of us. Inappropriate analogies with animal behavior when protecting territory, and the use of ambiguous terms (such as the expression "personal bubble") which imply that personal space is an individual characteristic, have a tendency to make us forget that we are always concerned with sociospatial behavior, which must be investigated both in relation to the physical environment and to the social situation and cultural limitations. These are the reasons for which Lecuyer proposes that we talk about interpersonal distance rather than personal space.

Canter discerns two other ambiguities. It is dangerous to interpret data about personal space only in terms of ergonomic variables, i.e., those controlling the information flow necessary to the relevant interpersonal relations. One must differentiate the space necessary in an ergonomic sense for the performance of certain tasks and for communication (this space is a function of anthropometry and physical properties), as well as the social use made of distance and proximity in the course of interpersonal relations. Hall's definition of four zones having different functions and describable by distances precise to the inch could encourage such confusion between necessity and social life. The other danger which Canter indicates is at the opposite extreme and consists of a bias toward the social determinants of personal space to the point of neglecting physical constraints. Many investigations cited by Canter have shown that people use the physical environment, and especially the built environment, to modulate their personal space. Thus, one cannot comment on the distances which people adopt in queues for trains without noting that whether studies were carried out in Japan, Britain, or in the United States, people always choose places near a pillar, outside the axes of movement, and with good visibility.

It is certainly necessary to take these remarks into account, but it remains clear that there can be no dispute about the heuristic value of the concept of sociospatial regulation of behavior. Altman and Vinsel (1977) reviewed 300 investigations which sought to identify the situational, social, and personal determinants of the distances observed between different people. These studies had been carried out in both the laboratory and the field, involved simulation by drawing and model, observations of sociospatial behavior in people placed in different conditions, or even, by analogy with Sommer's experiments, the direct investigation of individual reactions to intrusions into personal space.

The results of these investigations do not allow us to answer all the questions which can be raised. In particular, there is still insufficient information to test Hall's propositions about intercultural differences. Existing studies in this area are specific, not comparative, and it is difficult to generalize from the differences observed in groups with very dissimilar social status and in different experimental conditions. On the contrary, many constant effects have been observed across the sociospatial practices of groups with different ethnic and cultural backgrounds. In particular, it would seem that they use the personal, intimate, and public zones for the same sorts of behavior. One of the rare studies which are really comparative (Scherer, 1974) was concerned with the behavior of black and white children of matched social class in the schoolyard. There were larger interpersonal differences in middle-class children than in lower-class children, black or white. This suggests that differences which are hastily attributed to cultural or ethnic causes may in fact be due to social class.

Despite these gaps, research carried out recently on interpersonal distances has been sufficiently coherent for Altman and Vinsel to construct a summary table of results, which we will now discuss briefly.

Generally speaking, the research summarized allowed the existence of Hall's different zones and the uses to which they are put to be verified. Nevertheless, different distances were observed depending upon whether people were standing or seated: standing seems to relate to far-intimate and near-personal zones, while sitting seemed to be observed in the far-personal and near-social zones. In addition, Hall's hypotheses were verified by research into intrusion. When a subject who acted as an accomplice approached a stranger in a public place, the person intruded upon left the place or expressed vocally or nonverbally his annoyance and hostility. The closer the intrusion, the more rapid the departure. Yet the meaning which the person approached attributes to the invader's behavior also determines reaction. If the approach was threatening, and hostile intentions were attributed to the invader, the other person did not attempt to accommodate to the space which remained, but preferred to leave (Felipe and Sommer, 1966).

In other words, there are several possibilities for adaptation and reaction to intrusion, among which the subject chooses on the basis of his interpretation of the situation. In the same way, people forced by circumstances to be closer to other people than the norms would allow (for example, when a person has to use a narrow corridor in which two people are in conversation) only does so when it is impossible to do otherwise and compensates for this by verbal and nonverbal behavior and by averting his/her gaze.

There are many variables which influence the distance used in interpersonal relations. All of them involve the psychological interpretation of the situation, from both the point of view of the meaning of the controlled space and of the interpretation given to the behavior of the other people in the social situation which has thus been created. People who have a dominant position or who believe themselves to be dominant approach others more frequently than those who do not dominate or have less confidence in themselves. Another example concerns schizophrenics (who have a pathological tendency to exaggerate external threats). In a laboratory simulation (Horowitz et al., 1964), schizophrenics chose greater interpersonal distances than nonschizophrenics. Altman and Vinsel (1977) suggest that low "power," or the absence of control over the situation, are associated with increased interpersonal distance, while confidence, control, and authority reduce it. This is confirmed by the observations described above concerned with intrusion, in which it was seen that reaction was stronger when the stranger was threatening and of lower perceived importance. All of this is consistent, as Mercer (1975) has remarked, with tolerated or maintained distance between individuals being a method of filtering desired interpersonal contacts while retaining control of the situation.

These conclusions need to be placed in a wider framework. In fact, it is clear that the individual in a social situation can use other behaviors which would allow him to change the style of his interpersonal relations. Argyle and Dean (1965) and Argyle (1969, 1973) have shown the importance of gaze, information source, feedback, and social skill. They have put forward a model according to which there is an interdependence between verbal and nonverbal control. When some degree of intimacy is required, changes at the behavioral level (e.g., eye contact) will produce related changes in other behaviors (e.g., interpersonal distance). What is important is the balance established between the methods of control and the expression of psychological discomfort.

A variety of research has shown how well-founded this theory is. In particular, there is an interaction between gaze and proximity. Efram and Cheyne (1973) have shown this in the case of subjects who had to pass between two people in a narrow corridor. When doing so they lowered their eyes, averted their gaze, and thus avoided contact. Argyle and Dean (1965) observed subjects approaching people who were looking at them or even their photograph. Eye-contact was progressively lessened, so that at a distance of two feet they leaned forward, looked elsewhere, and scratched their head. When questioned, they expressed their discomfort. Patterson (1976) reviewed the research on compensatory mechanisms which give people control over the sociospatial environment. All the research reveals a relation between proximity and angle of interpersonal gaze. Further work will no doubt be able to show the precise nature of this balance and the variety of behaviors which come into play. The psychological importance of sociospatial regulation has been clearly demonstrated. If it were necessary to produce another example to support this, it would be that of the voluntary use made of sociospatial regulation in therapy: encounter groups, for example, in which contact with other people becomes the vehicle of greater self-awareness; and the relative positions of analyst and his patient, who is observed without himself seeing.

These three groups of investigations, territoriality, behavior in shared spaces, and personal space, have been developed in parallel and with aims which are very similar but in some ways different. All are concerned with relations between behavior in space and social relations, and with the use of space as a social expression or as a mode of relating to other people; in short, the way in which space is used, appropriated, and defended in a social context. The results are dissimilar because the problems were formulated differently, although there are points of clear similarity between the three fields of research. In the first place, all the sociospatial behaviors which have been investigated are reflections of the relation between the subject and others—his/her membership in certain groups, status, prestige in the sight of others, and the roles and functions which he/she fulfills. These also flow from the situation when the observation is made, and from this point of view it would not be possible to exaggerate the dynamic nature of this behavior. If the group changes, or its structure, or its aims, if the plans or the individual status of the subject are altered, then the spatial behavior will change also. It is not possible, therefore, to think in terms of the existence of a permanent zone of personal space which is characteristic of each individual and independent of the situation.

In the second place, behavior is a function of the physical environment and its resources, and will therefore differ according to material constraints, although these physical determinants do not of themselves dictate sociospatial behavior. The third point is more of a general question than a conclusion. A number of specific investigations indicate that different individuals placed in the same situation, who are relatively homogeneous with respect to social status, role, and so on, behave differently vis-à-vis space and its social implications. Neither the size of these differences nor the sources from which they arise are, however, at all well understood. At the most, it could be supposed that they relate to previous experiences of analogous situations and their effects, and to personality traits.

It is very probable that the possession of a space represents a necessary stage in the confirmation of the social and cultural identity of the individual, a concrete way of becoming aware of belonging to different groups and communities. From this point of view, it would be good to see some research into collective sociospatial behavior. A club without a meeting place, a family without a home, a religion without a place of worship, or a country without territory all show us that a group cannot exist without a spatial support. How does the group attachment to the spaces which are owned come into being? Which psychological factors are active, in addition to the obvious physical needs, in explaining defensive behavior toward intruders?

CHAPTER 5

Planning and Arranging the Environment

For the psychologist, the environment is not just external scenery, the location in which behavior takes place. All the problems dealt with in earlier chapters have emphasized the necessity for a transactional perspective. Perception and evaluation of the environment cannot be analyzed independently of the actions and behaviors of those who perceive and evaluate. It is, for example, behavioral adaptation to environmental stressors which determines the effects of stress; similarly, space and the control exercised over it are means of social expression. There is not a single aspect of environmental psychology in which the human being appears as passively subject to the force-fields of exterior influences. In addition, as was emphasized in the introduction, every psychologist concerned with environmental problems is insistent that the investigation of man-environment relations cannot be limited to the effects of the surroundings on the subject, but must also include the process of planning and arranging the environment, in which case the initiative comes back to the person.

The behaviors involved in arranging and planning are great in number and very diverse, indeed heterogeneous, in type. It is by these means that the individual changes the space available to him/her, according to various needs and preferences, whether it be one's office, the corner of a workshop, a bedroom, or the

141

study area in a student residence. It can also be carried out by a
group (family, class, or team) fitting out, furnishing, and decorating a house or apartment, lecture-room, workplace, or meeting room. In this context, it is obvious that the layout will result
from a process of negotiation, explicit or implicit. At the very
largest scale, the community plans institutions (hospitals, leisure centers, museums, schools, airports, and so forth), urban
developments, industrial zones, and parks. In all of these cases,
the relevant social processes vary according to whether it is a
matter of an individual, a restricted group, or members of a
more diffuse social category. In some instances where the community is not very organized, the planning process may provide
an occasion for it to become cohesive, to define its objectives, and
to choose its leaders and lines of action. There is evidence for
this in the great number of interest groups which come into
being when there are planning problems.

These types of behavior also show differing degrees of constraint, physical or technical. A submarine, for instance,
presents many more environmental constraints than a student's room, and a rented apartment more than an individual
house. There are also social and cultural constraints which, for
example, force the use of traditional forms and symbolic meanings, and which arouse the praise or condemnation of certain
styles of life. In spite of this diversity, there does seem to be a
general pattern which all planners seem to follow: the individual, the group, or the team of decision-makers arrive at a set of
objectives for the project and ensure that it is carried out on the
basis of their cognition (explicit, implicit, or even laid out in a
concrete or expert form) of these objectives and the correct way
of achieving them.

In these circumstances, one is led to wonder about the way in
which, in real terms, environmental planning forms a part of
applied psychology. Many other problems also seem to be directly relevant to the environment. There are philosophical
problems—there is not so much freedom in planning an environment that it can be treated like potter's clay. How, in view
of this, are individual freedom and environmental determinism
reconciled? There are also political and social problems when-

ever planning concerns a public facility or some part of the national or regional heritage. Who should make the decision? What participation process should be involved? Which objectives have priority? To what extent can a group of experts, by planning the environment, have an influence upon the lifestyle and behavior of the majority? In short, if philosophical, political, and social problems are clearly involved, as well as economic and biological ones, it remains to treat the psychological problems raised by planning much as they are treated by the psychologist, and in order to do this, to return planning to a psychological perspective.

The Skinnerian concept of operant conditioning and, perhaps more broadly, the sort of environmental ergonomics used in the design of workplaces provide one framework. Some environments can be projected with specific educational aims and constitute an ensemble of sources of positive and negative reinforcements, "a learning system organized so as to produce and maintain specific behavior topographies" (Studer, 1970). Environmental planning can in fact influence an individual to adopt adequate facilities. This is true in the case of safety equipment in the workplace and, for instance, the automatic closing of subway doors when the train is in motion. Behavior can also be acquired vicariously, e.g., by social imitation or by reading symbols. This is the way people learn to use pedestrian crossings, not to use one-way streets in the wrong direction, and to pay attention to a whole series of written or symbolized prohibitions.

But the planning of a restricted environment is not the only area which raises psychological problems. At a more basic level—that of man-environment relationships—it is necessary to take into account in environmental planning the individuals who are going to live, work, or spend their leisure in the planned environment and, more specifically, their needs, traditions, activities, and objectives. The organization of the environment, whether at the individual, family, group, or community level, is intended to match environmental resources with individual needs. This is, however, a flexible and dynamic process. In fact, the equilibrium which is required between the person and the environment is constantly in the process of being built up by the creation of specific environments and constantly degraded by changes in people, society, and technology. In addition, the process of environmental change is so slow that we always live in environments designed for the previous generation.

As Gump (1971) has reminded us, *synomorphous fit* (complementarity of form) is not limited to the ergonomic aspects mentioned above (fitting the design of the work-station to the behavior of the worker, or the size of the bed to the bodily posture of the sleeper). In the real world, however, no environment is designed in such a way that only one or two ranges of behavior are possible in it. Determinism is both broader and more flexible than that, and each and every environment is conceived so as to allow a limited, but still quite large, number of behaviors. Thus a laboratory, a store, a classroom, a bathroom, or a cinema does not determine behavior uniquely, but rather allows a well-defined set of possible behaviors. In just the same way, sitting posture depends upon the shape of the chair, without there being any specific and unique way of sitting in any one chair. The individual can always select the behavior which suits him best. At the limit, some behaviors can be deviant and still tolerated (e.g., eating a picnic lunch in the laboratory so as not to interrupt the work in process; improvising an entertainment for passengers in the subway; or using the bathroom to make very private phone calls). Environmental planning should therefore be directed, not at a strict determinism, but at allowing individuals to make a more or less limited choice within a range of possible behaviors compatible with the surroundings. We have already seen that environments impose a greater or smaller number of constraints, and that both the environment itself and social institutions sanction aberrant behaviors.

To take account of the correspondence between environmental and behavioral ensembles and the proposed aim of looking at the optimization of the man-environment relation, it is reasonable to borrow Michelson's (1977) term, "congruence." Congruence exists when the spatial parameters are not likely to prevent the desired behavior. This congruence can be mental, as when people judge that their environment is suitable for their desired activities, or experiential, when the context is that of the real, material optimization of the relationship between behavior and the environment. In short, as Michelson's formulation clearly shows, environmental planning (either by an individual for his own purposes, or by a small group with the users in view) does not consist of the restrictive application of a badly understood environmental determinism which would make a person the puppet of his environment. It is, on the contrary, the elaboration of a nonrestrictive environment which encourages those behaviors desired by the individual or the group and that facilitates the free actualization of specific intentions.

Described in this way, environmental planning clearly poses a set of psychological problems. In fact, if the way in which people act upon the external environment is seen from a strictly determinist point of view, then architectural research would need to receive special attention. As soon as the causality is seen as more flexible, environmental research takes in many psychological variables. A good example of this is given in Oscar Newman's book, *Defensible Space,* the subtitle of which *(Crime Prevention through Urban Design)* specifies its objectives. According to Newman, if one wishes to prevent vandalism or violence, it is not necessary to study the dysfunctions of the building design, nor to increase protective measures, surveillance, or the durability of the materials in use. What is essential is to build and plan the shared parts of neighborhoods and large blocks so that they "belong" (in the psychological sense) to the community, i.e., so that all the inhabitants feel themselves to be concerned with their use, maintenance, and protection. From a psychological point of view, Newman approaches the problem of vandalism in a way which assumes that violent behavior is not strictly determined by either the personality of the individuals or the characteristics of the environment. In another place, the same person would not behave as a vandal, since his behavior is the result of a way of perceiving the environment which is capable of analysis in terms of the man-environment relation.

It is convenient, therefore, to distinguish limitational environmental planning, designed to rigorously prohibit certain harmful or dangerous behaviors which raise cognitive and ergonomic problems, from the planning of a congruent environment, which imposes no specific limitations upon individual freedoms. This aspect raises at least four problems.

In the first place, there is very often a considerable gap between what users want and what architects and planners judge to be desirable. On this account, buildings are too often designed for a particular social class without taking into account the variation between subcultures, lifestyles, and even the social symbolism of the environment. The classical requirements of architecture are not sufficient to create congruence, and it is necessary to add to them an account of the needs and attitudes specific to each group of users. Architects perceive the external world in a way that differs from that of laymen. Thus, Canter (1969) has shown that the three most important aspects of a building, for architects, are coherence, character, and friendliness, while the last of these is not important to nonarchitects. It is a fact that many urban developments are rejected or criticized by their users because their planners had inaccurate or incomplete information about the needs, habits, and modes of living of the users. Describing these needs and explaining them in terms that can be used by the architect, and facilitating a harmony between the planner and the user are both, without a doubt, matters which raise a whole number of sociopsychological problems.

These problems would obviously be easy to solve if needs, hierarchies of values, and behavior were homogeneous and constant over time and place. One only has to glance around to see that this is not the case; the variety of life-styles, as Singer (1978) has emphasized, is quite evident when one considers individual timetables, hygiene habits, nutritional practices, entertainments, individual energy use, utilization of the built environment, or the way in which social indicators of the quality of life are ranked. Singer recommends the systematic study of time budgets and the use of technology in everyday life. Their variety reflects the variety in lifestyles and, more profoundly, the diversity of cultures and personalities. It is hardly necessary to point out that they are of concern to the psychologist.

A third phenomenon is a complicating factor in research on

man-environment congruence: the multifactor nature of environments, which has already been indicated by reference to Michelson (1977). Each set of surroundings has multiple functions. Whenever one aspect is modified, with a specific aim in view, it is impossible to avoid the introduction of other, unintended and unpredicted consequences. Thus, Parsons (1970), in an analysis of behavior in an open-plan school (i.e., one in which the pupils are not in separate classrooms but are grouped according to activity in a single large room, rather after the manner of a landscaped office), noted that the large rooms were not very noisy because of the absence of reverberation, but that it was nevertheless more difficult for the children to hear one another. Both pupils and teachers therefore had a tendency to come closer to one another, in both the physical and the psychological senses. As Ittelson (1973) commented, it is paradoxical that the open classroom should increase privacy, since it becomes more desirable despite the fact that the absence of walls to define a special place for each class ought to stimulate groups to break up. What is important in this case is more the predominant individual needs rather than the facilities available to them.

Hall (1966) put forward a novel explanation of the social behavior characteristic of the English upper class (distant, hiding all emotion, often rejecting conversaticn, and so forth). Since they were used, during infancy and adolescence, to living either in dormitories with low levels of privacy or in a nursery shared with their brothers and sisters, they developed attitudes which reduced free social exchange and allowed them to withdraw into themselves when they wanted to. When an American wishes to be alone, he goes to his bedroom and shuts the door, using the architectural features as his screen. The English, on the other hand, not having had individual rooms in childhood, have not learned to use space for solitary refuge. They have therefore internalized a number of barriers which others are assumed to understand.

In both of these cases, there appears to be some sort of indirect determinism. When the environment does not provide the facilities to satisfy individual or collective needs, individuals and groups develop behaviors intended to compensate for the environmental constraints or to create a social environment replacing or completing what is provided by the physical environment. These observations give a wider meaning to congruence: namely, specific behaviors adapted to environmental constraints so as to create the necessary equilibrium between the individual and his environment.

The fourth aspect of planning and arranging the environment with which psychology concerns itself is related to the perception by the individual of environmental causality. There are a number of cases in which the environmental determination of behavior, performance, or psychological development is not perceived as such by the lay person, either because it cannot be separated from the totality of the environment, the person concerned does not have relevant sensory apparatus for the important physical data, or perhaps because he projects feelings of comfort or discomfort upon particular factors. These facts have been available for a long time, at least as far as occupational psychology is concerned. At Hawthorne, Elton Mayo was called in as a consultant specifically because workers exposed to very low levels of illumination (comparable with moonlight) in an experimental workshop reported that their working conditions were excellent and that the lowered lighting level reduced visual fatigue. What they were evaluating in reality was predominantly the favorable social conditions (the interest shown in their environment, the fact of having been selected as experimental subjects, and the attention displayed toward their comfort). There are many analogous examples of this phenomenon in noise research.

Singer (n.d.) showed that children living in noisy homes were affected by their environment. Their differential sensitivity and their speed of learning to read were found to be disturbed. The mothers of these children, however, would certainly not have attributed the educational difficulties of their children to the ambient noise. This lack of knowledge of the psychological effects of the environment is even more striking when the causal factors are not directly perceptible, as is the case, for example, with the electrical properties of the atmosphere, the composition of the air, the bacteriological state of apparently clear water, and so on.

It is also necessary to take into consideration cases in which a group collectively projects its dissatisfaction upon an aspect of the environment that is really not at fault. A recent example of this concerns the reactions of the inhabitants of a suburb after the construction of a major road bordering their residential area. Strong complaints in respect to the traffic noise from those living alongside the road led to a noise survey being carried out, which showed that levels outside and inside the dwellings did not justify complaint. Interviews were then carried out in the complainants' households, which showed that the road separated a primary school from a substantial proportion of the homes of its pupils. A serious accident had recently injured several children on their way to school. It was therefore decided to build a footbridge over the road, which brought the complaints about noise to an end.

This differing capacity to identify environmental impact, or the precise source of annoyance, and to choose and arrange an environment to meet individual aims has been described by Steele (1973) as "environmental competence." He brought to our attention the fact that it is very often the case that negative and positive reinforcements are lacking or unclear. In addition, he suggested the possibility of specific education in the analysis of different aspects of the environment and how to experiment with their effects. The beginnings of this type of activity exist at the moment, using either model environments or questionnaires, upon whose results subjects are allowed to comment. In the same way that psychologists have developed professional orientations toward, for example, marriage counselling, it might perhaps be necessary to develop environmental counselling to help people wishing to choose or change their environment.

The planning and arrangement of the environment thus pose a whole number of psychological problems: how to inform planners about the real needs of the users, how to take into account the variation in individual preferences and their significance, how to predict the multiple results of environmental changes, and how to develop environmental competence. All of these factors have been the subject of recent field research. As is often the case for environmental psychology as a whole, however, we are most often concerned with specific work which is needed because of a limited question requiring immediate application of the results. In addition, these investigations relate to environments on different scales, from the disposition of personal spaces (bedrooms, offices) to urban planning, via the design and layout of institutional buildings such as hospitals, post offices, and schools.

By reviewing existing work, it can be seen that there are three different types of psychological problems within planning. The first of these concerns the behavior of the single individual, active in the environment, or if absolutely necessary, the behavior of a family unit. In these instances, behavior can be recorded in a variety of circumstances; choosing a house or a holiday resort, maintaining the home or place of work, spoiling or degrading different environments, planning them actively, or changing their appearance or organization. In all of these different cases, we are observing an individual or a family taking action to change their own environment. The interest for the psychologist lies in two different directions: the question of congruence, i.e., individuals' efforts to make their own, controllable sector of the environment match their needs; and the investigation of man-environment relations as a mode of analyzing personality, revealing the way in which people manage their environment, and of discriminating the symbolic value of the changes actually made.

The second type of psychological problem brings into play a set of different actors, those who play the key roles for large-scale planning—architects, planners, and community and city executives. Investigation of their activities largely centers upon empirical analysis of the adequacy of the relationship between buildings and the aims they were intended to fulfill, on the basis of their evaluation by the users.

The third type of problem brings together all the different people concerned with the environment, since it relates to attempts to bring the user and planner into communication with one another, either by giving citizens the means to participate in decision-making, or by attempting to describe their needs and preferences by the use of techniques which facilitate their expression (simulations, models, questionnaires). It is clear that this third category needs to base itself upon the results of the other two, and we shall attempt by way of concluding to clarify the underlying tendencies which they have in common. We shall start by examining the disparate contributions of each of these types of research.

THE INDIVIDUAL AND HIS PERSONAL ENVIRONMENT

Everybody, from the inhabitant of a suburban slum to the king in his palace, from the caveman to the tenant of a studio in one of the highrises of La Defense in Paris, has his own personal environment. How did he choose it? How does he arrange it? It is surprising to discover that the process of choosing a dwelling has only recently been subjected to investigation. Barrett (1976), a geographer, attempted to describe house-search behavior by analyzing the approaches used by a representative sample of families who had recently moved to Toronto. He showed that searches were short and restricted. In his sample, 50 percent of the people had searched for no more than a month, and 50 percent had visited no more than four houses before coming to a decision. In addition, each family only explored a limited geographical region, corresponding to their social class or ethnic origin. Bell (1968) had already emphasized the fact that residential mobility tends to lead to the relocation of movers among neighbors similar to themselves. He proposed three categories of lifestyle: the family, preferring detached houses away from the town center, and the consumption- and career-oriented, both of whom prefer to be near the center. Michelson (1977) questioned about 700 families who had just moved (also to Toronto) and distinguished the factors behind the move: lack of space, dissatisfaction with the neighborhood or type of dwelling, or change in place of work. The reasons for the choice of the new dwelling were utilizable space, layout of the dwelling, closeness to work, physical facilities, and modernity. As a whole, family factors and economic variables (especially the number and age of the children and whether the wife worked or not) seemed to be very important in the choice between an apartment in the center and a house and garden on the outskirts.

Other studies have approached the problem in a less direct manner by questioning various groups about their attitudes and needs with respect to housing. A number of points emerge from these investigations. First, a consensus in favor of a detached house with a little ground seems to be universal (Cooper, 1974). The question therefore arises as to whether city-dwellers are always going to be frustrated by being limited to an apartment which is often small. This does not always seem to be the case, at least for those who have always lived in that way: Sonnenfeld (1966) has shown that preferences are always biased in favor of the place of birth or somewhere one has lived for a long time. During the process of socialization, the individual learns cultural preferences. On this account, one could expect more critical judgments from migrants, or more generally, from those who have been forced to move. Even when the move is accompanied by an improvement in comfort, the previous house is still missed (Fried, 1963; Fried and Gleicher, 1961). The reasons given for this are interesting because they do not relate to the house itself, but to its environment. It is the district as a whole which creates a type of spatial identity. The informal relations which grow up with neighbors contribute to the creation of a social network to which the person belongs and that provides security, familiarity, and the sense of continuity.

A variation in preferences can also be seen beyond these social dimensions and the need for autonomy shown by the universal preference for the detached house. The choice of a dwelling is not the simple result of the economic capabilities and the material needs of a family. It is also the reflection of an individual's system of values. Rainwater (1966) brought to our attention the fact that attitudes toward housing vary with social class. At the very bottom of the scale, the inhabitants of urban slums seek as a priority a shelter in which to eat, sleep, and feel sure. The middle classes also aspire to security, but also look for features which ease the burden of housework. The highest classes have more complex attitudes because, in addition to all of these other functions, the house is for them the visible symbol of social and financial success.

Preferences with regard to the landscape and setting of the house have also been investigated, in a more sophisticated way. A number of researchers (notably Michelson, 1970 and Wohlwill, 1970) have analyzed the psychological dimensions underlying the preferences expressed. Environmental complexity, in particular, seems to be an important variable which can itself be broken down in a variety of ways according to the varied, unusual, or incongruous nature of the environment. It seems to be very clear that each individual has a personal inclination toward a given level of complexity. In general, however, a preference for complexity over excessively simple architectural schemes can be observed. Other variables seem to be involved in environmental choices, notably instrumentality (ease of access), esthetic quality, and social criteria.

Housing is not selected or desired, therefore, only because it has objective advantages. In just the same way, the manner in which the house is decorated and used is not solely determined by functional criteria. Even if the psychoanalytic and poetic interpretation (according to which each house has aspects—the interior which reflects the individual, and the facade representing a social mask; Cooper, 1974) is accepted with due caution, it must still be obvious that the way in which the dwelling is used has an affective and relational dimension. The social and cultural meaning of the dwelling has been especially emphasized by researchers using systematic observation. Rapoport (1969), for example, has compared the threshold of the house in various cultures. In the United States of America there is generally no barrier between the street and the garden, reflecting openness to other people. In England, on the other hand, the threshold is behind railings and gates. In the Moslem countries, privacy is even more strongly protected by the walls and locked doors which isolate the garden from the street. Similarly, Laumann and House (1972) made a comparison of the living rooms of 41

Detroit families of roughly equal income. Those decorated traditionally belonged to families which were well-established and whose parents came from the same sort of social position. Modern decor, on the other hand, was more often to be found among the socially mobile.

Zeisel (1971) investigated room-use in houses belonging to people of the same economic level but of different cultural background (middle-class Puerto Ricans in New York, white middle-class Americans, and American blacks from the South). He showed that the lifestyle, and especially the mode of relating to others, had a very strong influence on the organization of rooms. The kitchen, notably, had a hidden function for the Puerto Ricans, since it was the place in which the mother could show that she fulfilled her role efficiently. The more time she spent there, the more she gave the image of the ideal woman. Entry to the house was often gained via the kitchen, and meals were taken there; while the living room, a long way from the entrance, was a more solemn place where what Zeisel has dubbed the "family ikons" were displayed: children's certificates, wedding photos, or photos of politicians. Among the middle-class whites, the living room performed a social function and was the place where friends met. The kitchen was compact and had been transformed into a small laboratory, communicating directly with the living room so that the mistress of the house could carry out the duties of hospitality. Among Southern blacks, traditional cooking is spicy and aromatic, and meals were taken in the living room, the active center of family life.

Layout reflects lifestyle, and at work can be a way of imposing power structures. Hazard (1962) compared the arrangement of chairs, benches, and tables in Swiss, English, and U.S. courtrooms, and clearly showed that the relative height of the seats, the distance between the speakers, and the space reserved for the different participants reflected their roles and prerogatives. Thus, in the United States of America the equality of status between defense and prosecution is symbolized by the fact that their seats are of the same height and quality. On the other hand, in Geneva the prosecutor sits on the same platform as the judges, higher and in the best position to make himself heard by the defense counsel.

In Paris, in the lowest courts, the prosecuting magistrate sits upon an elevated platform, not as high as the judge's but higher than the advocate's. In Poland, the Gomulka reforms were translated into a modification of decor. Before, the prosecutor sat on the same level (and indeed at the same table) as the judges, so that he seemed, to the defense and the accused, to be a fourth judge. Nowadays, a gap has been introduced so that the prosecutor sits at the same height as the judges, but his table—and his role—are separated from those of the judges.

A more experimental study, reported by Joiner (1976), compared the ways in which offices are laid out in different organizations and by people who differ in status. The positions of the table, the visitor's seat, and the occupant were recorded in relation to the entrance to the office for university staff, officials, and business workers. University staff faced the door less often, and the private space they secured between the wall and the desk was generally larger than in the other two cases. Other factors also played a part in determining layout, especially status (in the private sector more senior people faced the door more frequently than their juniors) and the shape of the room (there was more door-facing in narrow rooms).

These investigations describe the factual situation, but in a more recent study Hansen and Altman (1976) longitudinally followed the process of arranging rooms in university residences as carried out by the students. They also looked at the links between these activities and academic results. They carefully recorded the objects introduced into the rooms by the students after two and after eleven weeks of residence. The objects were classified into six categories: personal objects (e.g., photographs of friends or relations); abstract messages (philosophical or religious); works of art; references (timetables, posters); entertainment objects (skis, radios); and objects the value of which was their link with personal activities (sporting pictures, for example). The total area of wall occupied by these objects was measured. The authors were able to conclude that while all students decorated their rooms, the area of wall used varied a great deal. By spring, 7 out of the 82 students in the sample had given up their studies. These 7 had used significantly less wall area and carried out significantly less decoration with personal objects.

The decoration, therefore, would seem to be a symbol of commitment to the institution, according to these investigators. This accords in a general way with the findings of other researchers which showed that the appropriation of space is associated with more effective functioning of the relevant groups.

In total, the selection, and then the layout and decoration of individual or family space reflect the relation between the person and the social environment. It is true that economic, material, and esthetic limitations have a role to play, but selection and decoration are also influenced by the culture of the social units to which the individual belongs or wishes to belong, to his style of life, and especially to the types of social relationships which he values with his neighbors, colleagues, and students; in short, with all those who take part in his social and professional life. Planning, layout, and decoration must therefore be seen above all as social behavior, since they represent a mode of structuring social relations, a socioenvironmental language, and a symbol of the integration of the individual with the social and institutional universe in which is found that portion of the space which is marked with his personality.

INSTITUTIONAL PLANNING

The problem of the influence of the environment on behavior is not just a subject for theoretical deliberation. The rapid development, over several decades, of large institutional buildings designed to meet precise objectives has given this problem an obvious importance. When approached by architects and planners, psychologists do not possess general principles allowing them to make exact recommendations about the size of offices, the layout of hospitals, or the right way to build a school. We have seen repeatedly that strict environmental determinism does not accord with the facts. Techniques for observing the behavior of users of institutional buildings have therefore been developed in the real world rather than the laboratory.

Is it really possible for a psychologist, on the basis of these observations, to participate usefully in the design of hospitals, schools, office blocks, and even prisons? Canter's (1975) comments on this are useful in reminding us that it is not as simple a matter as would at first seem to be the case, for a number of reasons. The first of these is that there are always two interactions, the influence of the building upon behavior and the influence of behavior on the building. This double interaction is all the more complex because of the tendency for the modification of the environment to vary between individuals and between environments. Second, Canter emphasizes that the role a person plays in the environment is a variable that directly influences his expectations of the environment and thus the interaction he has with it. There are two other points which merit attention. First, institutional environments are staffed and have hierarchical structures. The way in which the administrative team of a hospital behaves, for example, can cause very significant changes in the way in which the hospital building affects behavior. Second, the data which interest us here (user behavior in institutional buildings) change over time, and an observation limited to a particular moment in time could lead to unjustified generalization.

It will be useful to keep these cautions in mind as we examine the published research results. The importance of previous experience, of time, and of the role played is of help in understanding the apparent contradictions between the results obtained by those interested in room size in offices and, especially, the comparison between cellular and landscaped offices, where individuals' areas are defined only by plants and low screens. Nemecek and Grandjean (1973) questioned several hundred employees in fifteen landscaped offices. The advantages and disadvantages that they all mentioned showed a great deal of variation. Those who had previously worked in small offices seemed to be more sensitive to the limitations of their new environment, especially to the absence of privacy. Others were appreciative of the ease of work communications, and those of lower occupational status said that they were pleased with the liveliness of the landscaped office. Brookes and Kaplan (1972) studied the attitudes of 120 employees who had moved from an old cellular office into new landscaped offices. Although they complained about noise and frequent interruptions, they appreciated the esthetic quality of the new decor. Manning (1965) observed, in the same circumstances, that there was nostalgia for the old building, but that at the end of a year regret had given way to pride, and people appreciated the positive qualities of their offices. Zanadelli (1969) carried out the same type of study at the Ford Motor Company and assessed the change favorably, especially because of the disappearance of the "cave mentality," the obviousness of work circulation, the reduction in the heaps of closed files, and greater ease of communication.

A more objective investigation was carried out by Wells (1965), who compared 214 employees working in landscaped offices with 81 who occupied smaller areas by themselves or with 1 or 2 other people at an insurance company in Manchester, England. On the basis of the techniques of sociometric choice, he was able to make three observations. First, the choice of colleagues with whom one would prefer to work was related to the actual distance between the offices, with everybody wanting to work with people whom they already knew well and had worked with. Second, in the small offices people preferred members of the same section or department. Third, the number of isolates (i.e., people not selected by anybody) was greater in the small offices than in the landscaped offices. Despite the last finding, Wells concluded that the traditional environment was preferable because it guaranteed the internal cohesion of working teams, a necessary condition for their efficiency.

Canter (1968) paid attention to performance levels. He administered clerical aptitude tests to workers in either open plan offices (at least 100 people per room) or offices of the traditional sort (4 or 5 to a room). One group of subjects was tested in their own room, but at a desk other than their own; a second group was tested in a room either smaller or larger than their own. The results were very clear. The average level of performance was the same for the subjects who had been moved, but was inversely related to office size in the case of those who had been tested in their own rooms. It would therefore seem to be the case that room size exercises its influence on performance by a long-term process that was hidden in the first experimental procedure.

Observations made in *educational environments* have confirmed those of Canter and built upon them. Ittelson et al. (1974) traced the interesting history of school buildings, from the overcrowded classroom undifferentiated in age or curriculum, to the solemn academic buildings that serve to indicate the passive role of children, who are there only to receive the knowledge dispensed by the learned elders. New educational concepts have led to criticism of this idea. The school should not be a place where the child learns passively in an atmosphere more punishing than stimulating. In this case, the rigid, stark environment should surely change along with the educational methods. Many teachers and psychologists have thought so, but the experiments which exist do not seem to be conclusive. Sommer (1970) observed 23 different campuses and noted that students did in fact work in a great variety of places—libraries, their own rooms, and classrooms, but also cafeterias, lounges, halls and out-of-doors. The traditional classroom arrangement, with the teacher's desk facing those of the pupils, surely cannot be the only or the best one.

Experiments have been carried out on two variations in design, the first aiming to increase the stimulation received by the child in the classroom, and the second aimed at breaking up the traditional rigidity of furnishing. Animal psychologists have shown (see, for instance, Rosenzweig, 1966) that animals have better problem-solving capacities if they have been exposed to "rich" environments, as long as the variety of stimuli has not been excessive. There should be an optimum level somewhere between impoverished environments and overload conditions which are, as seen in the previous chapter, a cause of stress. But even when moderate, this environmental "richness" does not have a proven effect on school performance. Observations carried out over a whole year during a progressive process of enrichment gave no clear result (Busse et al., 1972). In addition, in some cases, like those of handicapped children, the pupil finds it easier to devote himself to the task if the environment is neutral and uninteresting.

The open-plan classroom, fairly frequent in England and more recently experimented upon in the United States of America, is a more systematic attempt to increase the physical activity of children and give them the freedom to follow their own interests and program themselves at their own speed. The open-plan classroom which, according to the Plowden Report, existed in half of English primary schools ten years ago, consists of small work areas organized around a free space in which children can jump, climb, and so on. In addition, each classroom has a library, a workshop, and a kitchen. Systematic observations of the behavior of children and teachers in these classrooms (Rivlin and Rothenberg, 1976; Brunetti, 1972) led to somewhat disappointing results. Everybody complained about the noise and the impossibility of being alone. In addition, although it was intended that the furniture should be moved about according to need, in all the classes observed by Rivlin, everything had been put in place at the beginning of the year and nothing was changed after that. Systematic analysis of the teachers' behavior showed that they were no more mobile than in the traditional class. They generally remained at their desks and it was the children who came to see them, to ask for help or to gather round the teacher for some group activity. The room was used in a very non-uniform way spatially. In some classes, half of the activities were carried out in a twelfth of the available area. The work carried out remained very individual. These difficulties were probably the result of excessive confidence in the effect of the environment alone. But the environment does not do the teaching. Students, teachers, and administrators need to get used to another method of education. The environment can only ease the adoption of different objectives, not impose them.

The planning and layout of hospitals also reflect the role that society wishes them to play. Spatial organization will clearly be thought about differently according to whether we are concerned with guarding the mentally ill and keeping them away from the healthy, or with nursing them. In this case as well, however, little is known and it is therefore necessary to test a priori assertions by putting specific decisions into effect and monitoring the results. By far the greatest number of these pieces of action research have been concerned with psychiatric hospitals, probably because the environments therein form part of the therapeutic process. Osmond (1957) in Canada, Bettelheim (1955) in the United States of America, and Sivadon et al. (1960) in France argued for hospital environments favorable to patients' return to a normal social life, and to feelings of safety and security in an enclosed space to which a person would be able to return if he/she wishes. It seems, in fact, that the social behavior of patients is influenced by the environment: Holahan and Saegert (1973) observed an increase in social behavior and a reduction in passive and isolate behavior after rearrangement of seats and partitions in multioccupied rooms. Ittelson et al. (1971) reported that behavioral changes in a psychiatric environment that had been partially redecorated extended beyond the area which had been renovated. The part fitted out with comfortable chairs no longer lent itself to single activities, and the patients used other rooms in which to be alone. The size of the rooms was also of importance, in that only having a small space available in a multioccupied room reduced freedom of choice and frequency of social behavior.

The hospital environment does, however, need to take account of the specific needs of different types of patient. Sommer (1969) has noted that it is necessary to satisfy the schizophrenic's need for isolation, and Bayes and Francklin (1971) have analyzed the difficulties encountered in planning a hospital for backward children. Izumi (1974), perceiving the necessity to put himself in the patient's place and to see the world as he/she would see it, decided to take LSD so as to see reality in a manner analogous with the schizophrenic's perception of it. In addition, environmental conditions can restrict the reactions of the medical and administrative authorities who could effect the desired changes in the environment. Rivlin and Wolfe (1972) have described the process of change in a psychiatric hospital for children in which, because the hospital was too large, they were able to gain access to parts of the building forbidden them. There had therefore developed a strict regime and programming of activities, predicated upon a concern for security and surveillance, which altered the free atmosphere characteristic of the therapy which the authorities wished to introduce. The conclusions of the investigators emphasized the way in which the environment can often have a strong influence upon institutional rules, which are independent of the people living in the institution and which will probably have a longer life than the conditions which brought them into being.

Old people's homes have also been subject to this type of research. Shared dormitories, vast dining rooms, and over-crowded sitting rooms which force elderly people to withdraw into themselves have all received criticism. As opposed to this, however, Lawton (1972) has emphasized the need to see the activity of others and the necessity of giving aged people the chance to place themselves near circulation ways. It is therefore dangerous to attempt to generalize from the results of any one study, since the problem is not always restricted to the environment. It is vital to take into account the rules of the institution, the degree of adaptation of old people to their segregation into an old people's world, and individual differences in the need for privacy (Schooler, 1976).

The problems raised by hospital and geriatric environments have parallels in the case of prisons. It is certainly the case that prisons have a primary repressive purpose. They also have environmental characteristics in common with other institutions, greater or lesser repression of personal initiative, living in single cells and in shared facilities, and the problems of rehabilitation. Research on the prison environment has made it clear that the limitation of activity and living in confined, drab, unvarying conditions produce the revolt and disorder which they are meant to prevent (Sommer, 1974).

Rehabilitation systems in which good behavior is rewarded by progressive environmental improvement (more privacy, less surveillance) have been criticized by Glaser (1972). He observed clearly that in the first two stages, the time that the prisoner devoted to work did increase. After this, however, the effect reversed and the leisure time increased, the intellectual level of entertainment went down, work occupied less time, and the prisoners gave up their efforts at occupational training. It would seem that by linking rehabilitation and the environment, the search for comfort had been more encouraged than had reform.

As a whole, these institutional investigations have given useful directions which were often unexpected but sometimes obvious. But it would be difficult not to be struck by the picture presented by the research. Psychologists have carried out observations of environmental effects under controlled conditions among schoolchildren, patients, old people, and prisoners. In some instances, they have also questioned the research subjects and made comparisons between survey results and objective data. In almost all cases there is the feeling of a stage play, with protagonists who do not speak. We know that there are differences between the needs of the users and the opinions of those who make the plans, between the residents' preferences and architectural canons, between the intended use and the actual use made of the built environment, but the ordinary citizen has only rarely a role to play in the planning process. How can this sort of cooperation happen?

PARTICIPATION IN PLANNING

Environmental planning was for a long time (and in the majority of cases is still) an autocratic process, the responsibility for which lay entirely with a group of experts. In addition, dwellings, institutional buildings, recreation areas, and parks are subject to regulations. It is only recently that the general public has been directly involved in some planning processes. The descriptions of participation in planning which it is possible to give, therefore, are often theoretical or at best founded upon isolated examples.

In reality, four categories of participation must be distinguished, all of which are quite different from a psychological point of view. The first type is "enforced" participation, in which the authorities try to impose upon the users certain modes of behavior with respect to the environment. Every environment is in fact modified by the simple fact of living or working there. The preservation of the existing situation implies the participation of the users. The second category, "passive" participation, has already been referred to in the chapter of this book concerned with environmental evaluation. It covers the attempts to explore the needs and wishes of users by surveys intended to clarify the way in which planners can take into account the opinions of the majority. "Active" participation breaks the pane of glass between users and planners, and is a dialogue which should take place at the design stage. This implies, for instance, that models and plans should be comprehensible to lay people. Finally, "spontaneous" participation arises when a group of users takes the initiative by making themselves heard and by seeking to impose their own will.

There is little to be said about enforced participation. In part this is because its objectives are often trivial (making people use litter bins in parks, making them keep off lawns and flower-beds), and also because the methods used are still very restricted in scope and interest. Study of these activities has concentrated upon behavioral techniques, essentially the description of the behavior exhibited when the experimenter manipulates environmental variables. Because of this, the research which has been carried out has produced solutions, the value of which has been experimentally demonstrated, but without our knowing the relevant motivations and psychological processes. If ever the solutions were ineffective, we would not know why and would have to start the research over from the very beginning.

Nonetheless, the literature (reviewed by Cone and Hayes, 1976) does show the pragmatic value of behavioral observation carried out systematically and its superiority to arbitrary, a priori decisions. It is therefore possible to select a text for litter bins which tells people not to throw garbage on the ground, or to choose positions of chairs and benches which would prevent access to lawns except for those who wished to sit there, or to identify the types of rewards which would encourage children to pick up litter. But we would still need to know the nature of the attitudes toward these types of pollution and what the determinants are of feelings of collective responsibility in this area. Do the same sorts of people watch others pollute or degrade the environment, and take part in these activities, and when the opportunity is presented commit acts of vandalism? It has been observed that pollution and graffiti are more common in environments which are already polluted or which have been badly maintained. If this is true, is it true of all people, in all types of environments? According to an article by Crump et al. (1977) this does not seem to be the case, since they were able to observe walkers in a forest clearing the places in which they wished to picnic.

If enforced participation does not rely upon psychological analyses which are sufficiently extensive, then encouraging passive participation must bring into play extremely sophisticated methods of attitudinal analysis. Two distinct approaches have been followed. The first consists of elaborating the survey instruments by which meaning is investigated and that can be used as a test for defining the preferences and attitudes of individuals or groups. The second aims to define the social indicators which allow us to measure different aspects of the quality of life, how they change, and how they relate to other social indicators and economic indices. Although both methods rely on increasing the sophistication of questionnaires, defining the psychological dimensions which they measure, and using them to describe various segments of the population, the difference between the two approaches is clear. The first describes preferences and tendencies, even an "environmental personality," while the second relates to levels of satisfaction with the environment.

The Environmental Preference Questionnaire (EPQ) was introduced by Rachel Kaplan in 1970 and is still undergoing development. It has the great merit of being extremely short. It consists of 6 questions, each of which corresponds to an area of interest relating to 60 examples which the subject evaluates by means of a 6-point scale. For example, Question 5 asks for the importance attributed by the subject to the following problems:

- population
- law and order
- inflation
- the generation gap
- environmental decline.

A number of factor analyses have produced six separate scales: taste for nature; desire for romantic escape; modern development; preference for the suburbs; social interests; passive reaction to stress; and taste for the city (Kaplan, 1977). The EPQ has been used to differentiate between homogeneous groups characterized by a definite environmental role: amateur gardeners, or residents in the same community.

The Environmental Response Inventory (McKechnie, 1977) consists of 184 statements about everyday environmental problems (e.g., "I like to do my shopping in a store where everything is well displayed"). The subject responds by means of a 5-point scale expressing degree of agreement with the statement. Its present form is the result of a series of factor analyses and the classification of items by different judges, which have led to 8 basic dimensions, each made up of between 19 and 22 items. The scales are: pastoralism, urbanism, environmental adaptation, stimulus-seeking, environmental trust, antiquarianism, need for privacy, and mechanical orientation—to which has been added a validity scale which checks the honesty of the responses. The ERI aims to define and measure the way in which individuals interact with their environment. Since its construction in 1972, the ERI has been applied to a large number of problems: the characteristics of migrants, and the differentiation of groups of students whose subjects would be expected to produce varying orientations to the environment (geographers, planners) or of groups of respondents with different leisure activities (e.g., people who visited nature parks).

Social indicators can be used to check the efficiency of environmental planning and the degree of satisfaction with the proposed objectives—the whole process therefore aiming at that optimization of the man-environment relationship which is the primary aim of environmental psychology. We are obviously concerned here with subjective indicators (the subjects' own expressions of their living conditions) as opposed to objective indicators such as income data, house size, household equipment, or health statistics (Campbell, 1976).

Several different methods of evaluating these subjective indicators have been tried in the last ten years (reviewed by Mann, 1977). It is not possible to make a comparison between them or to discuss their significance here in any detailed way, but one of the most interesting studies was carried out by Andrews and Withey at Michigan University's Institute for Social Research (1976). On the basis of a careful review of previous survey results and a series of interviews, they drew up a list of 123 items in the form of a questionnaire covering every aspect of life. Each of these is assessed by respondents on a 7-point scale which runs from "delighted" to "terrible." General well-being was assessed in a number of ways and its relation to different aspects of the quality of life investigated. It is not possible to summarize in a few lines all of their results and their use in the analysis of the quality of life of contrasting samples of the American population. They show great variability in satisfaction levels for all the variables investigated, and the existence of three areas of general satisfaction in which response ran from positive to negative: first, private life (children, marriage, family, friends); then, those parts of life shared with neighbors and colleagues; and third, public problems (cost of living, taxes, government activities, and national problems). The enormous amount of work carried out by Andrews and Withey greatly exceeds a purely environmental framework, but it does involve a methodology which is applicable to the validation of planning and shows the links between different aspects of well-being.

The examples given above are not related to occasions on which real participation took place. Nonetheless, it is possible to believe that active participation in the planning and design of the built environment would increase the satisfaction of the users, in the same way as that in which participation in decision-making facilitates the execution of decisions by the participants. If participation in planning is rare, it is probably because there are so many obstacles to it. The first of these is certainly the lack of interest on the part of those citizens for whom the environment concerned is not strictly their personal one. An interesting study by Tucker (1978) showed how variable is the feeling of being concerned with the environment. It also revealed, implicitly, that it is an elite which feels that it is concerned, since the attitude is linked to age, income, social status, and perceived power over one's fate. Eisemon (1975) has proposed the use of the Truax technique to mitigate the passivity and avoid the elitism in participation. The obstacle which has to

be overcome, however, is that of expertise: architectural drawings do not mean a great deal to laypersons, and the desires of
users lack clarity and realism. The Truax technique is a simulation in the form of a game, constructed in order to facilitate the
putting to rights of a building complex called Truax. The participants were given the responsibility of building a scale model of
their ideal home. Once the respondents had become familiar
with the symbols for the different parts of the apartment, they
played with the financial restraints; i.e., they received a total
budget and a price for each element. When the game was over,
respondents discussed their model dwelling with the architect.

Another way of proceeding would be to use more or less sophisticated simulations to present realistic and detailed models,
in three dimensions and color, of planning and architectural
schemes. Examples of this technique are the automobile simulator of UCLA in which the "driver" is able to see the road and
landscape unroll before him, and the REAL, a British simulator
at the Transport and Road Research Laboratory, in which spectators in a "living room" see a simulated landscape through a
window, with the appropriate sound effects. The simulator at
Berkeley, which we have already mentioned in connection with
its use in experiments on the perception and evaluation of the
environment, can make use of a miniaturized landscape and a
mobile camera providing a detailed film of what the landscape
would be like.

None of these approaches is simply a costly game. They are
the only available method of presenting designs to the un-
trained in such a way that they can be perceived clearly and
compared with the proposed alternatives. When planning projects are not submitted to those who have interests in them, it
can happen that they spontaneously form groups and demand to
be consulted or to alter a project in the course of design. Groups
of this type have multiplied rapidly in France, and it would be
interesting to know which social and environmental contexts
are especially favorable to their development. Goodman and
Clary (1976) asked this question in relation to Los Angeles International Airport. Six neighboring communities were subject
to equal disturbance because of the extension of one of the run-

ways in 1967, but the community reactions varied a great deal, from total passivity to extreme activism. A representative sample was questioned in each community, and the responses showed that active protest was not related only to noise level, but also to social and psychological factors. These included the level of annoyance, the misfeasance attributed to the airport managers, social status, and length of residence in the community. Another element which was not described here but which is certainly of importance, is the presence of leaders in the community who will take the initiative to form a group to speak for the community.

Environmental planning raises a series of psychological problems which we have been able to describe briefly here. The research which has been carried out on these practical matters is disparate in nature and often excessively narrow in scope. Nonetheless, one theme has emerged as of some permanence and in more clarity than in the other chapters: individual differences. The arrangement and design of personal places, the choice of dwelling, reactions to institutional living, level of concern, and hierarchy of environmental preferences are all dimensions within which people vary and differentiate themselves from others. These differences, in addition, are neither random nor inexplicable. The designers of tests, like Kaplan and Mc-Kechnie, have found groups with different environmental personalities in the same way as there are typologies of planning, and studies that allow us to speculate that environmental participation is the result of specific experiences and social affiliations. In addition, surveys have shown the existence of common preference hierarchies in homogeneous groups. All these types of research must be continued in order to improve our understanding of the relation between the variety of environments and the diversity of people.

Conclusion

Two types of comments appear repeatedly in the previous chapters. On the one hand, all the themes have occasioned pessimistic remarks regarding the possibilities of synthesis and of constructing general models. This conclusion is echoed by many writers, as is clear in the first chapter. Environmental psychology will have to construct theoretical schemes, but they are at the moment rare, and those which do exist are provisional and fragmentary. On the other hand, however, there is a certain note of optimism which runs through all the research, the feeling that it is useful and necessary, that the new field is fertile, that not only do the field studies have the stamp of realism and authenticity, but they will proceed to revive and encourage the progress of traditional psychology. It is obvious, and perhaps has been throughout, that there is a lack of fit between these two evaluations of environmental psychology. Which attitude should we adopt? If the pessimistic, then we must fear that environmental psychology will always remain a purely empirical discipline. If the optimistic, then we should assess its original contribution.

Although dissonant, both of these attitudes are justified, and each is explained by two reasons, the negative and the positive characteristics of environmental psychology.

THE NEGATIVE ASPECT

(1) Environmental psychology suffers from a lack of integration of the objective and the subjective study of the environment

or, more simply, of the techniques borrowed from experimental psychology and those from social psychology. In all of the themes dealt with here, results can be divided into two categories: for example, the effects of noise on performance and the subjective annoyance caused by noise; distance perception and environmental cognition; behavioral effects of density and social needs; environmental conditioning and the study of preferences for different environments; and so on. As long as there is no attempt to analyze subjective reactions in the light of behavioral data and, conversely, to take behavior (adaptation, planning, response) into account in interpreting attitudes, choices, and reported annoyance, environmental psychology will develop in two mutually exclusive directions.

(2) The practical nature of the problems of environmental psychology has been accused of giving the subject an anecdotal character. The superficial appearance of some results has often been explained in terms of the immediate utility of those results. These excuses are not totally necessary. For a start, what was true ten or even five years ago need not be true today. Many pieces of research have been carried out specifically to increase knowledge: Lee on the neighborhood, Canter on distance perception, Singer on the effects of noise, Craik on environmental personality, Stokols on density, and so on. On the other hand, it is clear that the majority of experimental studies are strictly descriptive or narrowly specific. Most often, associations between behavior and environment are described, or comparisons are made between the different environmental behaviors of different groups. But it is rare that the comparisons are sufficiently broad or sustained to allow the creation of explanatory hypotheses.

THE POSITIVE ASPECT

(1) The transactional approach exercises increasing domination over research and interpretation. In other words, it is not the physical environment which is studied, but the environment as perceived, evaluated, and relevant to each individual. There is a parallel in occupational psychology. The variety of

individual motivations cannot be understood until account is taken of the fact that each individual carries out, in his own way, an evaluation of his inputs and outputs. Thus, the feeling of justice or equity is purely subjective, since it is a function of comparison between oneself and others, one's contribution and the return from the organization. In just the same way, the environment has a unique character for every individual and it is as a function of individual interpretation of the environment (the estimated risks, the control the individual believes he has, the comparison of expectations and reality, or the threatening or reassuring character of the environment) that actions are taken and adaptations made. The transactional approach does not constitute an extreme case of individualism. In fact, present-day research shows quite clearly that identical experiences, a common culture, and the availability of the same information will lead to a similar reading of the environment. It is therefore unnecessary to become resigned to fundamental idiosyncrasy at the individual level. We must instead develop a differential psychology based on the comparison of subgroups that are homogeneous in culture, experience, information, and aspirations.

(2) Finally, there are the theoretical gaps. Theories are, however, built from new concepts. This first step is under way. From this point of view, the creativity of environmental psychologists is striking. There are a great number of new concepts which are still becoming clearer in meaning: information overload, environmental site, overmanning, learned helplessness, proxemics, crowding and territoriality, privacy, personal space, and so on. Some of these concepts are so new as not yet to have found adequate translation into French. One can perhaps look forward to a reduction of the difficulties encountered in building theoretical models with the aid of a traditional theoretical apparatus, perhaps borrowed from general psychology and architecture, when a set of scientific meanings has been given to the new environmental vocabulary.

Bibliography

I. GENERAL WORKS

ALTMAN, I. (1975) Environment and Social Behavior. Belmont, CA: Brooks/Cole.

BARKER, R.G. (1968) Ecological Psychology. Stanford, CA: Stanford University Press.

CANTER, D. (1977) The Psychology of Place. London: Architectural Press.

——— (1975) Environmental Interaction. London: Surrey University Press.

——— (1970) The Place of Architectural Psychology. Pittsburgh, PA: Edra Two.

DOWNS, R. and D. STEA [eds.] (1973) Image and Environment. Chicago: Aldine.

HALL, E.T. (1966) The Hidden Dimension. New York: Doubleday.

HEIMSTRA, N.W. and L.H. McFARLING (1974) Environmental Psychology. Belmont, CA: Brooks/Cole.

ITTELSON, W.H. [ed.] (1973) Environment and Cognition. New York: Seminar Press.

——— H.M. PROSHANSKY, L.G. RIVLIN, and G. WINKEL (1974) An Introduction to Environmental Psychology. New York: Holt, Rinehart & Winston.

LEE, T.R. (1976) Psychology and the Environment. London: Methuen.

MEHRABIAN, A. and J.A. RUSSELL (1974) An Approach to Environmental Psychology. Cambridge, MA: MIT Press.

MERCER, C. (1975) Living in Cities. Middlesex, Eng.: Penguin.

MICHELSON, W. (1970) Man and His Urban Environment: A Sociological Approach. Reading, MA: Addison-Wesley.

PORTEOUS, J.D. (1977) Environment and Behavior: Planning and Everyday Urban Life. Reading, MA: Addison-Wesley.

SAARINEN, T. (1976) Environmental Planning, Perception and Behavior. Boston: Houghton Mifflin.

SOMMER, R. (1969) Personal Space: The Behavioral Basis of Design. London: Prentice-Hall.

STEELE, F. I. (1973) Physical Settings and Organization Development. Reading, MA: Addison-Wesley.

II. BIBLIOGRAPHIES

CRAIK, K. H. (1973) "Environmental psychology." Annual Review of Psychology 24: 403-422.

———— (1970) "Environmental psychology," in New Directions in Psychology, Vol. 4. New York: Holt, Rinehart & Winston.

STOKOLS, D. (1978) "Environmental psychology." Annual Review of Psychology 29: 253-295.

WOHLWILL, J. (1970) "The emerging discipline of environmental psychology." American Psychologist 25, 4: 303-312.

III. COLLECTED READINGS

ALTMAN, I. and J. WOHLWILL [eds.] (1977) Human Behavior and Environment, Vol. 2. New York: Plenum Press.

———— (1976) Human Behavior and Environment, Vol. 1. New York: Plenum Press.

BAUM, A., J. E. SINGER, and S. VALINS [eds.] (1978) Advances in Environmental Psychology. New York: Erlbaum.

CRAIK, K. H. and E. H. ZUBE, [eds.] (1976) Perceiving Environmental Quality. New York: Plenum Press.

DOWNS, R. M. and D. STEA [eds.] (1973) Image and Environment. Chicago: Aldine.

GUTMAN, R. [ed.] (1972) People and Buildings. New York: Basic Books.

MICHELSON, W. [ed.] (1975) Behavioral Research Methods in Environmental Design. Stroudsburg: Halsted Press.

MITCHELL, W. J. [ed.] (1972) Environmental Design: Research and Practice. Los Angeles, CA: University of California Press.

PREISER, W. F. E. [ed.] (1973) Environmental Design Research. Stroudsburg: Dowden, Hutchinson & Ross.

PROSHANSKY, H., W. ITTELSON, and L. G. RIVLIN (1976) Environmental Psychology, 2nd Ed. New York: Holt, Rinehart & Winston.

STOKOLS, D. (1977) Perspectives in Environment and Behavior. New York: Plenum Press.

WAPNER, S., S. B. COHEN, and B. KAPLAN [eds.] (1976) Experiencing the Environment. New York: Plenum Press.

WOHLWILL, J. and D. H. CARSON [eds.] (1972) Environment and the Social Sciences: Perspectives and Application. Washington, DC: American Psychological Association.

IV. CITED BOOKS AND ARTICLES

ACKING, C. A. (1974) Evaluation of Planned Environment. Document D7. Stockholm: National Swedish Institute for Building Research.

———— and R. KÜLLER (1972) "The perception of an interior as a function of its colour." Ergonomics 15, 6: 645-654.

ADELBERG, B. (1979) "Activity ranges of children in urban and ex-urban communities." University of Kansas (unpublished).

ALTMAN, I. and W.W. HAYTHORN (1967) "The ecology of isolated groups." Behavioral Sciences 12: 169-182.

ALTMAN, I. and A.M. VINSEL (1977) "Analysis of Hall's proxemics framework," ch. 5 in Human Behavior and Environment, Vol. 2. New York: Plenum Press.

ALTMAN, I., D.A. TAYLOR, and L. WHEELER (1971) "Ecological aspects of group behavior in social isolation." Journal of Applied Social Psychology 1: 70-100.

ALTMAN, I., P.A. NELSON, and E.E. LEFT (1972) "The ecology of home environments," in Catalog of Selected Documents in Psychology. Washington, DC: American Psychological Association.

AMES, A. (1951) "Visual perception and the rotating trapezoidal window." Psychological Monographs 65, 324.

ANDREWS, F.M. and S.B. WITHEY (1976) Social Indicators of Well-being. New York: Plenum Press.

APPLEYARD, D. (1973) " Notes on urban perception and knowledge," ch. 6 in R. Downs and D. Stea (eds.) Image and Environment. Chicago: Aldine.

ARCHER, J. (1970) "Effects of population density on rodents," in J.H. Crook (ed.) Social Behaviour in Birds and Mammals. New York: Academic Press.

ARDREY, R. (1966) The Territorial Imperative. New York: Atheneum.

ARGYLE, M., (1973) Social Interaction. Harmondsworth, Eng.: Penguin.

———— [ed.] (1969) Social Encounters. Harmondsworth, Eng.: Penguin.

———— and I. DEAN (1965) "Eye contact, distance and affiliation." Sociometry 28: 289-304.

BARKER, R.G. and H. WRIGHT (1955) The Midwest and Its Children: The Psychological Ecology of an American Town. New York: Row & Peterson.

BARRETT, F. (1976) "The search process in residential relocation." Environment & Behavior 8, 2: 169-198.

BATCHELOR, J.P. and G.R. GOETHALS (1972) "Spatial arrangements in freely formed groups." Sociometry 35, 2: 270-279.

BATTRO, A.M. and E.J. ELLIS (1972) "Estimation subjective de l'espace urbain." Année Psychologique 1: 39-52.

BAUM, A. and S. VALINS (1977) Architecture and Social Behavior. Hillsdale, NJ: Erlbaum.

BAYES, K. and S. FRANCKLIN [eds.] (1971) Designing for the Handicapped. London: G. Godwin.

BECKER, F.D. (1973) "Study of spatial markers." Journal of Personality and Social Psychology 26, 3: 439-445.

BELL, W. (1968) "The city, suburb and a theory of social choice," in S. Greer (ed.) The New Urbanization. New York: St. Martin.

BELOFF, J. and H.L. BELOFF (1961) "The influences of valence on distance judgment of human faces." Journal of Abnormal Psychology 62: 720-723.

BENNETT, C.A. and P. REY (1972) "What's so hot about red?" Human Factors 14: 149-154.

BETTELHEIM, B. (1955) Truants from Life. New York: Free Press.

BORSKY, P.N. (1961) Community Reactions to Air Force Noise. Dayton, OH: WADD Technical Report 60-689.

BOYCE, P. R. (1975) "The luminous environment," ch. 4 in D. Canter (ed.) Environmental Interaction. London: Surrey University Press.

BRENNAN, T. (1948) Midland City. London: Dobson.

BREWSTER SMITH, M. (1977) "Some problems of strategy in environmental psychology," in D. Stokols (ed.) Perspectives in Environment and Behavior. New York: Plenum Press.

BRIGGS, R. (1973) "Urban cognitive distance," ch. 19 in R. Downs and D. Stea (eds.) Image and Environment. Chicago: Aldine.

_____ (1973) "On the relationship between cognitive and objective distance," in W. F. E. Preiser (ed.) Environmental Design Research. Stroudsburg: Dowden, Hutchinson & Ross.

BROADBENT, D. E. (1963) "Differences and interaction between stresses." Quarterly Journal of Experimental Psychology 15: 205-212.

_____ (1957) "Effects of noise of high and low frequency on behaviour." Ergonomics 1: 21-28.

_____ (1954) "Some effects of noise on visual performance." Quarterly Journal of Experimental Psychology 6: 1-16.

_____ and E. A. J. LITTLE (1960) "Effects of noise reduction in a work situation." Occupational Psychology 34: 133-142.

BROADY, M. (1966) "Social theory in architectural design." Architectural Association Journal 81: 149-154.

BRONZAFT, A. L. and D. P. McCARTHY (1975) "The effect of elevated train noise on reading ability." Environment & Behavior 7, 4: 517-527.

BROOKES, M. and A. KAPLAN (1972) "The office environment: space planning and effective behaviors." Human Factors 14: 373-391.

BROWN, I. D. and E. C. POULTON (1961) "Measuring the spare 'mental capacity' of car drivers by a subsidiary task." Ergonomics 4: 35-40.

BRUNER, J. S. (1966) "On cognitive growth," in J. S. Bruner et al. (eds.) Studies in Cognitive Growth. New York: John Wiley.

_____ (1957) "On going beyond the information given." Contemporary Approaches to Cognition. Cambridge, MA: Harvard University Press.

_____ and C. C. GOODMAN (1947) "Value and need as organizing factors in perception." Journal of Abnormal Social Psychology 42: 33-44.

BRUNETTI, F. A. (1972) "Noise distraction and privacy in conventional and open school environments," in W. J. Mitchell (ed.) Environmental Design: Research and Practice." Los Angeles: University of California Press.

BRUNSWIK, E. (1956) Perception and the Representative Design of Psychological Experiments. Los Angeles: University of California Press.

BURTON, I. (1972) "Cultural and personality variables in the perception of natural hazards," in J. F. Wohlwill and D. H. Carson (eds.) Environment and the Social Sciences: Perspectives and Application. Washington, DC: American Psychological Association.

_____ R. W. KATES, and G. F. WHITE (1968) The Human Ecology of Extreme Geographical Events. Toronto: University of Toronto.

BUSSE, T. V., M. REE, M. GUTRIDE, T. ALEXANDER, and L. S. POWELL (1972) "Environmentally enriched classrooms and the cognitive and perceptual development of negro preschool children." Journal of Educational Psychology 63: 15-21.

CALVIN, J.S., J.A. DEARINGER, and M.E. CURTIN (1972) "An attempt of assessing preferences for natural landscapes." Environment & Behavior 4: 447-470.

CAMPBELL, A. (1976) "Subjective measures of well-being." American Psychologist 31: 117-124.

—— P. CONVERSE, and W. RODGERS (1976) The Quality of American Life. New York: Russell Sage Foundation.

CANTER, D. (1975) "Buildings in use," in D. Canter (ed.) Environmental Interaction. London: Surrey University Press.

—— (1974) "Empirical research in environmental psychology: a brief review." Bulletin of the British Psychological Society 27 (April): 31-37.

—— (1974) "Psychological determinants of errors in distance estimation in cities." Bulletin of the British Psychological Society 27: 95.

—— (1971) The Development of Scales for the Evaluation of Buildings. Glasgow: University of Strath Clyde.

—— (1969) "An intergroup comparison of connotative dimensions in architecture." Environment & Behavior: 37-88.

—— (1968) "Office size: an example of psychological research in architecture." Architect's Journal: 881-888.

—— and S. CANTER (1971) "Close together in Tokyo." Design and Environment 2: 60-63.

CANTER, D. and S. TAGG (1975) "Distance estimation in cities." Environment & Behavior 7, 1: 59-80.

CANTER, D. and R. WOOLS (1970) "A technique for the subjective appraisal of buildings." Building Sciences 5: 187-198.

CANTER, D., J. BROWN, and H.P. RICHARDSON (1976) Study of House Buying. Guildford, Eng.: Housing Research Unit.

CANTER, D., S. WEST, and R. WOOLS (1974) "Judgments of people and their rooms." British Journal of Social and Clinical Psychology 13: 113-118.

CARLESTAM, G. and L. LEVI (1973) "Urban conglomerates as psychosocial human stressors," cited in W.H. Ittelson (ed.) Environment and Cognition. New York: Seminar Press.

CARP, F.M. and ZADAWASKI, R.T. (1976) "Dimensions of urban environment quality." Environment & Behavior 8, 2: 199-239.

CARPENTER, A. (1962) "The effect of noise on work." Annals of Occupational Hygiene 1: 42-54.

CHAPIN, F.S. and R.K. BRAIL (1969) "Human activity systems in the metropolitan United States." Environment & Behavior 1, 2: 107-130.

CHEIN, I. (1954) "The environment as a determinant of behavior." Journal of Social Psychology 39: 115-127.

CHOMBART de LAUWE, P.H. (1976) Espaces d'Enfants. Paris: Ministère de la qualité de la vie.

—— (1965) Des Hommes et des Villes. Paris: Payot.

—— (1959) Famille et Habitation. Paris: CNRS.

CHRISTIAN, J.J., V. FLYGER, and D.E. DAVIS (1960) "Factors in the mass mortality of a herd of Sika deer." Chesapeake Science 1: 79-96.

CICCETTI, C.J. (1972) "A multivariate statistical analysis of wilderness users in the U.S.," in J.V. Krutilla (ed.) Natural Environments. Baltimore, MD: Johns Hopkins University Press.

COHEN, S. (1978) "Environmental load and the allocation of attention," in A. Baum et al. (eds.) Advances in Environmental Psychology. New York: Erlbaum.

———— and A. LEZAK (1977) "Noise and inattentiveness to social cues." Environment & Behavior 9, 4: 559-572.

COHEN, S., D.C. GLASS, and J.E. SINGER (1973) "Apartment noise, auditory discrimination and reading ability in children." Journal of Experimental Social Psychology 9: 407-422.

COHEN, S., D.C. GLASS, and S. PHILLIPS (1979) "Environment and health," in N.E.F. Freeman (ed.) Handbook of Medical Sociology. Englewood, NJ: Prentice-Hall.

CONE, J.D. and S.C. HAYES (1976) "Applied behavior analysis and environmental problems," in I. Altman and J.F. Wohlwill (eds.) Human Behavior and Environment, Vol. 1. New York: Plenum Press.

COOPER, C. (1974) "The house as a symbol of the self," in J. Lang (ed.) Designing for Human Behavior. Stroudsburg: Dowden, Hutchinson & Ross.

CORCORAN, D.W.J. (1962) "Noise and loss of sleep." Quarterly Journal of Experimental Psychology 14: 178-182.

CRAIK, K. (1976) "The personality research paradigm in environmental psychology," ch. 4 in S. Wapner et al. (eds.) Experiencing the Environment. New York: Plenum Press.

CRONBACH, L. (1975) "Beyond the two disciplines of scientific psychology." American Psychologist 30, 2: 116-128.

CRUMP, S.L., D.L. NUNES, and E.K. CROSSMAN (1977) "The effects of litter on littering behavior in a forest environment." Environment & Behavior 9, 1: 137-147.

DAVIES, A.D. and D.R. DAVIES (1975) "The effects of noise and time of day upon age differential interference at two checking tasks." Ergonomics 18: 321-386.

DAVIS, G. and V. AYERS (1975) "Photographic recording of environmental behavior," in W. Michelson (ed.) Behavioral Research Methods in Environmental Design. Stroudsburg: Halsted Press.

DEAN, R.D. and C.L. McGLOTHLEN (1975) "Effects of combined heat and noise on human performance," in D. Canter (ed.) Environmental Interaction. London: Surrey University Press.

DeJONGE, B. (1962) "Image of urban areas: their structure and psychological foundations." Journal of the American Institute of Planners 28: 266-275.

DESOR, J.A. (1972) "Toward a psychological theory of crowding." Journal of Personality and Social Psychology 21: 79-83.

DOHRENWEND, B.S. and B.P. DOHRENWEND (1972) "Psychiatric disorders in urban settings," in G. Caplan (ed.) American Handbook of Psychiatry. New York: Basic Books.

DUBOS, R. (1965) Man Adapting. New Haven, CT: Yale University Press.

EDNEY, J. J. (1974) "Human territoriality." Psychological Bulletin 81, 12: 959-973.

EFRAM, M. G. and J. A. CHEYNE (1974) "Affective concomitants of the invasion of shared space: behavioral, psychological and verbal indicators." Journal of Personality and Social Psychology 29: 219-226.

———— (1973) "Shared space: the cooperative control of spatial areas by two interacting individuals." Canadian Journal of Behavioral Science 5: 201-210.

EISEMON, T. (1975) "Simulations and requirements for citizen participation in public housing." Environment & Behavior 7, 1: 99-123.

EOYANG, C. K. (1974) "Effects of group size and privacy in residential crowding." Journal of Personality and Social Psychology 30: 389-392.

ESCHENBRENNER, A. J. (1971) "Effects of intermittent noise on the performance of a complex psychomotor task." Human Factors 13: 59-63.

ESSER, A. H. (1970) "Interactional hierarchy and power structure on a psychiatric ward: ethological studies of dominance behavior in a total institution," in S. J. and C. Hutt (eds.) Behavioral Studies in Psychiatry. Oxford: Pergamon Press.

———— A. S. CHAMBERLAIN, E. D. CHAPPLE, and N. S. KLINE (1965) "Territoriality of patients on a research ward," in J. Wortis (ed.) Recent Advances in Biological Psychiatry, Vol. 7. New York: Plenum Press.

EYSENCK, H. (1967) Fact and Fiction in Psychology. London: Penguin.

FARIS, R. E. L. and H. W. DUNHAM (1939) Mental Disorders in Urban Areas. Chicago: University of Chicago Press.

FELDMAN, R. (1968) "Response to compatriot and foreigner who seek assistance." Journal of Personality and Social Psychology 10: 202-214.

FELIPE, N. J. and R. SOMMER (1966) "Invasions of personal space." Social Problems 14, 2: 206-215.

FINKELMAN, J. M. and D. C. GLASS (1970) "Reappraisal of the relationship between noise and human performance by means of a subsidiary task measure." Journal of Applied Psychology 54: 211-213.

FLYNN, J. E., T. J. SPENCER, O. MARTYNIVIK, and C. HENDRIK (1973) "Interim study of procedures for investigating the effect of light on impression and behavior." Illuminating Engineering Society Journal 3: 87-94.

FORBES, G. and H. GROMOLL (1971) "The lost letter technique as a measure of social variables: some exploratory findings." Social Forces 50: 113-115.

FRANCES, R. (1963) La Perception: Que Sais-je? Paris: Presses Universitaires de France.

FRANCESCATO, D. and W. MEBANE (1973) "How citizens view two great cities: Milan and Rome," in R. Downs and D. Stea (eds.) Image and Environment. Chicago: Aldine.

FREEDMAN, J. L. (n.d.) "Population density, juvenile delinquency and mental illness in New York City." Commission on Population Growth and the American Future, Vol. 7, pp. 515-523.

———— S. KLEVANSKY, and P. I. EHRLICH (1971) "The effect of crowding on human task performance." Journal of Applied Social Psychology 8: 528-548.

FRIED, M. (1963) "Grieving for a lost home," in L. J. Duhl (ed.) The Urban Condition. New York: Basic Books.

_____ and P. GLEICHER (1961) "Some sources of residential satisfaction in an urban slum." Journal of the American Institute of Planners 27, 4: 250-264.

GALL, O. R., W. R. GOVE, and J. M. McPHERSON (1972) "Population density and pathology: what are the relationships for man?" Science 176, 1: 23-30.

GIBSON, J. E. (1966) The Senses Considered as Perceptual Systems. Boston: Houghton Mifflin.

_____ and R. D. WALK (1960) "The visual cliff." Scientific American 202: 64-71.

GLASER, D. (1972) "Architectural factors in isolation promotion in prisons," in J. F. Wohlwill and D. H. Carson (eds.) Environment and the Social Sciences: Perspectives and Application. Washington, DC: American Psychological Association.

GLASS, D. C. and J. SINGER (1972) Urban Stress. New York: Academic Press.

_____ and L. N. FRIEDMAN (1969) "Psychic cost of adaptation to environmental stressors." Journal of Personality and Social Psychology 12: 200-210.

GLASS, D. C., J. E. SINGER, and J. W. PENNEBAKER (1977) "Behavioral and physiological effects of uncontrollable environmental events," in D. Stokols (ed.) Perspectives in Environment and Behavior. New York: Plenum Press.

GLASS, D. C., J. E. SINGER, H. S. LEONARD, D. S. KRANTZ, S. COHEN, and H. X. CUMMINGS (1973) "Perceived control of aversive stimulation and the reduction of stress responses." Journal of Personality 41: 577-595.

GLASSMAN, J. B., B. R. NURKHART, and G. G. GRANT (1978) "Density, expectation and extended task performance." Environment & Behavior 10, 3: 299-317.

GOFFMAN, E. (1971) Relations in Public. New York: Basic Books.

_____ (1959) The Presentation of Self in Everyday Life. New York: Doubleday.

GOLANT, S. and I. BURTON (1969) "Avoidance response to the risk environment," in Natural Hazard Research. Working paper No. 6. Toronto: Toronto University Press.

GOLDMAN, R. and J. W. SANDERS (1969) "Cultural factors and hearing." Exceptional Child 35: 489-490.

GOLEDZINOWSKI, F. (1976) "L'espace du metro: etude du comportement des voyageurs en matiere d'orientation." Le Travail Humain 39, 1: 43-53.

GOODCHILD, B. (1974) "Class differences in environmental perception: an exploratory study." Urban Studies 11, 2: 157-169.

GOODMAN, R. F. and B. B. CLARY (1976) "Community attitudes and action in response to airport noise." Environment & Behavior 8, 3: 441-469.

GOUGH, H. G. (1965) "Conceptual analysis of psychological test scores and other diagnostic variables." Journal of Abnormal Psychology 70: 294-302.

GRAEVEN, D. B. (1975) "Necessity, control and prediction of noise annoyance." Journal of Social Psychology 95: 85-90.

GREEN, R. G. and P. C. POWERS (1971) "Shock and noise as instigating stimuli in human aggression." Psychological Reports 28: 983-985.

GREEN, R. G. and E. C. O'NEAL (1969) "Activation of cue-elicited aggression by general arousal." Journal of Personality and Social Psychology 11: 289-292.

GRIFFITHS, I.D. (1975) "The thermal environment," in D. Canter (ed.) Environmental Interaction. London: Surrey University Press.

———— and P.R. BOYCE (1971) "Performance and thermal comfort." Ergonomics 14: 457-468.

GRIFFITT, W. (1970) "Environmental effects on interpersonal affective behavior: ambient effective temperature and attraction." Journal of Personality and Social Psychology 15: 240-244.

———— and R. VEITCH (1971) "Hot and crowded: influences of population density and temperature on interpersonal affective behavior." Journal of Personality and Social Psychology 17: 92-98.

GUMP, P. (1971) "Milieu, environment and behavior." Design and Environment 2, 4: 48-52.

———— and B. ADELBERG (1978) "Urbanism from the perspective of ecological psychologists." Environment & Behavior 10, 2: 171-192.

HANSEN, W.B. and I. ALTMAN (1976) "Decorating personal places." Environment & Behavior 8, 4: 491-505.

HART, R. and G.T. MOORE (1973) "The development of spatial cognition: a review," ch. 14 in R. Downs and D. Stea (eds.) Image and Environment. Chicago: Aldine.

HASTORF, A.H., D.J. SCHNEIDER, and J. POLEFKA (1970) Perception. Reading, MA: Addison Wesley.

HATWELL, Y. (1974) De l'Espace Corporel a l'Espace Ecologique. Paris: Presses Universitaires de France, pp. 133-141.

HAYES, S.C. and J.C. CONE (1977) "Decelerating environmentally destructive lawn walking." Environment & Behavior 9, 4: 511-534.

HAZARD, J. (1962) "Furniture arrangement as a symbol of judicial roles." Review of General Semantics 19, 2: 181-188.

HEDIGER, H. (1962) "The evolution of territorial behavior," in S. Washburn (ed.) The Social Life of Early Man. London: Methuen.

HEIMSTRA, N.W. and L.H. McFARLING (1974) Environmental Psychology. Belmont, CA: Brooks/Cole.

HEINEMEYER, W.F. (1967) "The urban core as a centre of attraction," in E.J. Brik (ed.) Urban Lore and Inner City. Leiden.

HIGH, T. and E. SUNDSTROM (1977) "Room flexibility and space use in a dormitory." Environment & Behavior 9, 1: 81-90.

HIROTO, D.S. and M.E.P. SELIGMAN (1975) "Generality of learned helplessness in man." Journal of Personality and Social Psychology 31:311-327.

HOLLINGSHEAD, A.B. and F.C. REDLICH (1952) Social Class and Mental Illness. New York: John Wiley.

HOLMBERG, I. and D.P. WYON (1969) "The dependence of performance in school on class room temperature." Educational Psychological Interaction 31.

HOLOHAN, C.J. and S. SAEGERT (1973) "Behavioral and attitudinal effects of large-scale variation in the physical environment of psychiatric ward." Journal of Abnormal Psychology 82: 454-462.

HOROWITZ, M.J., D.F. DUFF, and L.D. STRATTON (1964) "Body buffer zone." Archives of General Psychiatry 11, 6: 651-656.

HUMPHREYS, M. A. (1977) "Relating wind, rain and temperature to teachers' reports of young people's behavior," in D. Canter (ed.) The Psychology of Place. London: Architectural Press.

HUTEAU, M. (1975) "Un style cognitif: la dépendance-indépendance à l'égard du champ." Année Psychologique 75: 197-262.

HUTT, C. and J. J. VAIZEY (1966) "Differential effects of group density on social behavior." Nature 209: 1371-1372.

ITTELSON, W. (1960) Some Factors Influencing the Design and Function of Psychiatric Facilities. New York: Brooklyn College.

––––––– K. A. FRANCK, and T. J. O'HANLON (1976) "The nature of environmental experience," in S. Wapner et al. (eds.) Experiencing the Environment. New York: Plenum Press.

ITTELSON, W., H. PROSHANSKY, and L. RIVLIN (1971) "Bedroom size and social interaction of the psychiatric ward." Environment & Behavior 2, 3: 255-270.

ITTELSON, W., L. RIVLIN, and H. PROSHANSKY (1976) "The use of behavioral maps in environmental psychology," in H. Proshansky et al. (eds.) Environmental Psychology. New York: Holt, Rinehart & Winston.

IZUMI, K. (1974) "LSD and architectural design," cited in W. Ittelson et al. (eds.) An Introduction to Environmental Psychology. New York: Holt, Rinehart & Winston.

JACCARD, P. (1932) Le Sens de Direction et l'Orientation Lointaine chez l'Homme." Lausanne: Payot.

JAY, P. (1968) "The interior environment: sense and nonsense." Architectural Review (February).

JOINER, D. (1976) "Social ritual and architectural space," in H. Proshansky et al. (eds.) Environmental Psychology. New York: Holt, Rinehart & Winston.

KAPLAN, S. (1977) "Patterns of environmental preference." Environment & Behavior 9, 2: 195-217

––––––– (1973) "Cognitive maps in perception and thought," ch. 4 in R. Downs and D. Stea (eds.) Image and Environment. Chicago: Aldine.

––––––– (1973) "Cognitive maps, human needs and the design environment," in W. F. E. Preiser (ed.) Environmental Design Research. Stroudsburg: Dowden, Hutchinson & Ross.

––––––– (1972) "The challenge of environmental psychology: a proposal for a new functionalism." American Psychologist 27, 2: 140-143.

KATES, R. W. (1962) Hazard and Choice Perception in Flood Plain Management. Chicago: University of Chicago Press.

KIRMEYER, S. (1978) "Urban density and pathology." Environment & Behavior 10, 2: 247-269.

KITTEL, G. and H. G. DIEROFF (1971) "Problème de la modification du sens des couleurs sous l'influence du bruit." Zentralblatt fuer Verkehrsmedizin 3: 184.

KLEIN, D. C., E. FENCIL-MORSE, and M. E. P. SELIGMAN (1976) "Learned helplessness, depression and the attribution of failure." Journal of Personality and Social Psychology 33, 5: 508-516.

KOFKA, K. (1935) Principles of Gestalt Psychology. New York: Harcourt Brace Jovanovich.

KORMAN, A. K. (1971) Industrial and Organizational Psychology. Englewood Cliffs, NJ: Prentice-Hall.

KORTE, C. and N. KERR (1975) "Response to altruistic opportunities under urban and rural conditions." Journal of Social Psychology 95: 183-184.

KORTE, C., I. YPMA, and A. TOPPEW (1975) "Helpfulness in Dutch society as a function of urbanization and environmental input level." Journal of Personality and Social Psychology 32: 996-1003.

KRANTZ, D. S., D. C. GLASS, and M. L. SNYDER (1974) "Helplessness, stress level and the coronary-prone behavior pattern." Journal of Experimental Social Psychology 10: 284-300.

KRUTILLA, J. U. [ed.] (1972) Natural Environments. Baltimore, MD: Johns Hopkins University Press.

LAUMANN, E. and J. HOUSE (1972) "Living-room styles and social attributes," in E. Laumann (ed.) The Logic of Social Hierarchies. Chicago: Markham.

LAURENDEAU, M. and A. PINARD (1968) Les Premières Notions Spatiales de l'Enfant. Paris: Delachaux et Niestlé.

LAWTON, M. P. (1972) "Some beginning of an ecological psychology of old age," in J. F. Wohlwill and D. H. Carson (eds.) Environment and the Social Sciences: Perspectives and Application. Washington, DC: American Psychological Association.

LAZARUS, R. S. and J. B. COHEN (1977) "Environmental stress," in I. Altman and J. Wohlwill (eds.) Human Behavior and Environment, Vol. 2. New York: Plenum Press.

LECRET, F. and M. POTTIER (1971) "La vigilance, facteur de sécurité dans la conduite automobile." Le Travail Humain 34: 51-68.

LECUYER, R. (1976) "Adaptation de l'homme à l'espace, adaptation de l'espace à l'homme." Le Travail Humain 39, 2: 195-206.

——— (1975) "Psychosociologie de l'espace." Anée Psychologique 75: 549-573.

——— (1974) "Rapports entre l'homme et l'espace." (unpublished)

LEE, T. (1971) "Psychology and architectural determinism." Architect's Journal 154: 253-262, 475-483, 651-659.

——— (1970) "Perceived distance as a function of direction in a city." Environment & Behavior 2, 1: 40-51.

——— (1968) "Urban neighborhoods as a socio-spatial schema." Human Relations 21, 3: 241-268.

LEVY, M. (1977) "Overpopulation, concentration, dispersion." Population et Sociétés 10 (April).

LEVY-LEBOYER, C. (1977) Etude Psychologique du Cadre de Vie. Paris: CNRS.

——— B. VEDRENNE, and M. VEYSSIERE (1976) "Psychologie différentielle des gênes dues au bruit." Année Psychologique 76: 245-256.

LEWIN, K. (1951) Field Theory in Social Science. New York: Harper & Row.

——— (1948) Resolving Social Conflicts. New York: Harper & Row.

——— (1946) "Action research and minority problems." Journal of Social Issues 2: 34-46.

——— (1936) Principles of Topological Psychology. New York: McGraw-Hill.

——— (1935) A Dynamic Theory of Personality. New York: McGraw-Hill.

LEWIS, O. (1959) Five Families. New York: Mentor Books.

LIPMAN, A. (1967) "Chairs as territory." New Society 20: 564-566.

LITTLE, B.R. (1972) Person-Thing Orientation: A Provisional Manual for the T-P Scale. Oxford: Oxford University Press.

LITTON, R. (1972) "Aesthetic dimensions of landscape," in J.U. Krutilla (ed.) Natural Environments. Baltimore, MD: Johns Hopkins University Press.

LONG, A.J. (1973) "Territorial stability and hierarchical formation." Small Groups Behavior 4, 1: 56-63.

_____ (1971) "Dominance-territorial criteria and small group structure." Comparative Group Studies 2: 235-265.

_____ (1970) "Dominance-territorial relations in small groups." Environment & Behavior 2: 190-191.

LOO, C.M. (1973) "The effects of spatial density on the social behavior of children." The Journal of Applied Psychology 57, 4: 372-381.

LORENZ, K. (1969) L'aggression. Paris: Flammarion.

LOWENTHAL, D. and M. RIEL (1972) "The nature of perceived and imagined environments." Environment & Behavior 42: 189-207.

_____ (1972) "Environmental structures: semantic and experiential environments." Publications in Environmental Perception 8.

LOWREY, R.A. (1973) "A method for analyzing distance concepts of urban residents," in R. Downs and D. Stea (eds.) Image and Environment. Chicago: Aldine.

_____ (1971) "Distance concepts of urban residents," in J. Archea and C. Eastman (eds.) Proceedings of the Second EDRA Conference, Carnegie Mellon University, Pittsburgh.

LUCAS, R.C. (1974) "User concepts of wilderness and their implications for resource management," cited in N.W. Heimstra and L.H. McFarling (eds.) Environmental Psychology. Belmont, CA: Brooks/Cole.

LUNDBERG, V. (1973) "Emotional and geographical phenomena in psychophysical research," ch. 17 in R. Downs and D. Stea (eds.) Image and Environment. Chicago: Aldine.

_____ O. BRATFISCH, and G. EKMAN (1972) "Emotional involvement and subjective distance: a summary of investigations." Journal of Social Psychology 87: 169-177.

LYMAN, S.M. and M.B. SCOTT (1965) "Territoriality: a neglected sociological dimension." Social Problems 15, 2: 236-249.

LYNCH, K. (1960) The Image of the City. Cambridge, MA: MIT Press.

MACKWORTH, N.H. (1950) "Researches on the measurement of human performance." Medical Research Council Report No. 268. London: Her Majesty's Stationery Office.

MANDLER, G. (1962) "From association to structure." Psychological Review 69: 415-427.

MANN, S.H. (1977) "The use of spatial indicators in environmental planning," in I. Altman and J.F. Wohlwill (eds.) Human Behavior and Environment, Vol. 2. New York: Plenum Press.

MANNING, P. [ed.] (1965) Office Design: A Study of Environment. Liverpool: The Pikington Research Unit.

MARANS, R. (1970) Planned Residential Environments. Ann Arbor, MI: Institute for Social Research.

MARSHALL, N.J. (1972) "Privacy and environment." Human Ecology 1: 93-110.

MASON, J.W. (1976) "Selectivity of corticosteroid and catecholamine responses to various natural stimuli," in G. Servan (ed.) Psychology of Human Adaptation. New York: Plenum Press, pp. 147-171.

MATTHEWS, K.E. and L.K. CANON (1975) "Environmental noise level as a determinant of helping behavior." Journal of Personality and Social Psychology 32: 571-577.

MAURER, R. and J.C. BAXTER (1972) "Image of the neighborhood and city among Black-, Anglo-, and Mexican-American children." Environment & Behavior 4: 351-388.

McGREW, P.L. (1970) "Social and spatial density effects on spacing behavior in pre-school children." Journal of Child Psychology and Psychiatry 11: 197-205.

McKECHNIE, G.E. (1977) "The Environmental Response Inventory in application." Environment & Behavior 9, 2: 255-277.

_____ (1977) "Simulation techniques in environmental psychology," ch. 7 in D. Stokols (ed.) Perspectives in Environment and Behavior. New York: Plenum Press.

_____ (1974) Manual for the Environmental Response Inventory. Palo Alto, CA: Consulting Psychologists Press.

MERRENS, M. (1973) "Nonemergency helping behavior in various sized communities." Journal of Social Psychology 90: 327-328.

MICHELSON, W. (1977) Environmental Choice, Human Behavior and Residential Satisfaction. New York: Oxford University Press.

_____ (1977) "From congruence to antecedent conditions: a research for the basis of environmental improvement," ch. 9 in D. Stokols (ed.) Perspectives in Environment and Behavior. New York: Plenum Press.

_____ and P. REED (1975) "The time budget," ch. 5 in W. Michelson (ed.) Behavioral Research Methods in Environmental Design. Stroudsburg: Halsted Press.

MILGRAM, S. (1976) "The experience of living in cities," in H.M. Proshansky et al. (eds.) Environmental Psychology. New York: Holt, Rinehart & Winston.

_____ and D. JODELET (1976) "Psychological maps of Paris," ch. 8 in H.M. Proshansky et al. (eds.) Environmental Psychology. New York: Holt, Rinehart & Winston.

MILLER, J.G. (1964) "Adjusting to overloads of information," in D. McKrioch and E.A. Weinstein (eds.) Disorders of Communication. Baltimore, MD: Williams & Wilkins.

MILLER, W.R. and M.E. SELIGMAN (1973) "Depression and learned helplessness in man." Journal of Abnormal Social Psychology 84: 228-238.

MISCHEL, W. (1973) "Toward a cognitive social learning reconceptualization of personality." Psychological Review 80: 252-238.

MITCHELL, R. E. (1974) "Affect among the poor of Hong Kong and other cities," in W. C. Ittelson et al. (eds.) An Introduction to Environmental Psychology. New York: Holt, Rinehart & Winston.

MOORE, R. J. and E. E. FELLER (1971) "Seating preferences: preliminary investigations." Psychological Reports 21: 1073-1074.

MOOS, R. H. (1976) "Conceptualizations of human environment," ch. 3 in H. Proshansky et al. (eds.) Environmental Psychology. New York: Holt, Rinehart & Winston.

—————— (1969) "Sources of variance in responses to questionnaires and in behavior." Journal of Abnormal Psychology 74: 405-412.

MUNROE, R. L. and R. H. MONROE (1972) "Population density and effective relationships in three East African societies." Journal of Social Psychology 88: 15-20.

MURRAY, R. (1977) "The influence of crowding on children's behavior," in D. Canter (ed.) The Psychology of Place. London: Architectural Press.

NEMECEK, J. and E. GRANDJEAN (1973) "Results of an ergonomic investigation of large space offices." Human Factors 15:111-124.

NEWMAN, O. (1972) Defensible Space. New York: McMillan.

NEWSON, J. and E. NEWSON (1968) Four Years Old in an Urban Community. London: Penguin.

ORLEANS, P. (1973) "Differential cognition of urban residents: effects of social scale on mapping," ch. 7 in R. Downs and D. Stea (eds.) Image and Environment. Chicago: Aldine.

OSMOND, H. (1957) "Function as the basis of psychiatric ward design." Mental Hospital 8: 23-29.

PAGE, R. A. (1977) "Noise and helping behavior." Environment & Behavior 9, 3: 311-314.

PAILHOUS, J. (1970) La Représentation de l'Espace Urbain. Paris: Presses Universitaires de France.

PARSONS, H. M. (1970) "Human factors in environmental design: the state of the art." Presented to the Human Factors Society.

PATTERSON, M. L. (1976) "An arousal model of intimacy." Psychological Review 3: 235-245.

PEPLER, R. D. (1963) "Performance and well-being in heat," in Temperature: Its Measurement and Control in Science and Industry. New York: Van Nostrand Reinhold.

PETRESCU, L. (1969) "Le bruit et la mémoire." Atomes 270: 691.

PIAGET, J., P. FRAISSE, E. VURPILLOT, and R. FRANCES (1963) "La perception, t. VI," in P. Fraisse and J. Piaget (eds.) Traité de Psychologie Expérimentale. Paris: Presses Universitaires de France.

PIERON, H. (1955) La Perception. Paris: Presses Universitaires de France.

PLOWDEN, R. (1967) Children and Their Primary Schools. London: Her Majesty's Stationery Office.

PLUTCHIK, R. (1959) "The effects of high intensity intermittent sound on performance, feeling and physiology." Psychological Bulletin 56: 133-151.

POCOCK, O. C. D. (1977) "Urban environmental perception and behavior," in D. Canter (ed.) The Psychology of Place. London: Architectural Press.

POULTON, E. C. and D. McKERSLAKE (1965) "Effects of warmth on perceptual efficiency." Aerospace Medicine 36: 29-34.

PROSHANSKY, H. M. (1976) "Environmental psychology: a methodological orientation," ch. 5 in H. M. Proshansky et al. (eds.) Environmental Psychology. New York: Holt, Rinehart & Winston.

_____ and T. O'HANLON (1977) "Environmental psychology, origins and development," in D. Stokols (ed.) Perspectives in Environment and Behavior. New York: Plenum Press.

PROSHANSKY, H. M., W. H. ITTELSON, and L. G. RIVLIN (1976) "Freedom of choice and behavior in a physical setting," in H. Proshansky et al. (eds.) Environmental Psychology. New York: Holt, Rinehart & Winston.

PROVINS, K. A. (1966) "Environmental heat, body temperature and behavior: an hypothesis." Australian Journal of Psychology 18: 118-129.

RAINWATER, L. (1966) "Fear and the house-as-haven in the lower class." Journal of the American Institute of Planners 32, 1: 23-31.

RAPOPORT, A. (1975) "Towards a redefinition of density." Environment & Behavior 2: 133-158.

_____ (1969) House Form and Culture. Englewood Cliffs, NJ: Prentice-Hall.

RAWLS, J. R., R. E. TREGO, C. N. McGAFFEY, and D. J. RAWLS (1972) "Personal space as a predictor of performance under close working conditions." Journal of Social Psychology 86, 2: 261-267.

REUCHLIN, M. (1977) Psychologie. Paris: Presses Universitaires de France.

RIVLIN, L. G. and M. ROTHENBERG (1976) "The use of space in open classrooms," in H. Proshansky et al. (eds.) Environmental Psychology. New York: Holt, Rinehart & Winston.

RIVLIN, L. G. and M. WOLFE (1972) "The early history of a psychiatric hospital for children: expectations and reality." Environment & Behavior 4, 1: 31-71.

ROBINSON, I. M., W. G. BAER, T. K. BANERJEE, and P. G. FLASHBART (1975) "Trade-off games," in W. Michelson (ed.) Behavioral Research Methods in Environmental Design. Stroudsburg: Halsted Press.

RODIN, J. (1976) "Density, perceived choice and response to controllable and uncontrollable outcomes." Journal of Experimental Social Psychology 12: 564-578.

ROETHLISBERGER, F. J. and DICKSON, W. J. (1939) Management and the Worker. Cambridge, MA: Harvard University Press.

ROGLER, L. H. (1967) "Slum neighborhoods in Latin America." Journal of Inter-American Studies 9, 4: 507-528.

ROHE, W. and Q. H. PATTERSON (1975) "The effects of varied levels of resources and density on behavior in a day care center," cited in I. Altman (ed.) Environment and Social Behavior. Belmont, CA: Brooks/Cole.

ROSENMAN, R.H., M. FRIEDMAN, R. STRAUSS, M. WURM, C.D. JENKINS, and H.B. MESSINGER (1966) "Coronary heart disease in the western collaborative group study: a follow-up of two years." Journal of the American Medical Association 196: 130-136.

ROSENZWEIG, M.R. (1966) "Environmental complexity, cerebral change and behavior." American Psychologist 21: 321-332.

ROSS, H.L. (1961) "Reasons for moves to and from a central city area." Social Forces 40: 261-263.

RYD, H. and D.P. WYON (1970) Methods of Evaluating Human Stress due to Climate. National Swedish Institute for Building Research, No. 06/70.

SAARINEN, T.S. (1973) "The use of projective techniques in geographical research," in W. Ittelson (ed.) Environment and Cognition. New York: Seminar Press.

_____ (1966) Perception of the Drought Hazard on the Great Plains. Chicago: University of Chicago Press.

SAEGERT, S. (1976) "Stress-inducing and reducing quality of environments," in H. Proshansky et al. (ed.) Environmental Psychology. New York: Holt, Rinehart & Winston.

SCHACHTER, S. (1959) The Psychology of Affiliation. Stanford, CA: Stanford University Press.

SCHERER, S. (1974) "Proxemic behavior of primary school children as a function of their socio-economic class and subculture." Journal of Psychiatry and Social Psychology 29: 800-805.

SCHMID, C. (1970) "Urban crime areas: part II." American Sociological Review 25: 655-678.

_____ (1969) "Urban crime areas: part I." American Sociological Review 25: 527-542.

SCHMITT, R.C. (1966) "Density, health and social disorganization." Journal of the American Institute of Planners 32: 438-440.

_____ (1957) "Density, delinquency and crime in Honolulu." Sociological and Social Research 41: 274-276.

SCHOOLER, K.K. (1976) "Environmental change and the elderly," in I. Altman and J.F. Wohlwill (eds.) Human Behavior and Environment, Vol. 1. New York: Plenum Press.

SELIGMAN, M.E.P. (1975) Helplessness: On Depression, Development and Death. San Francisco: Freeman.

SELYE, H. (1956) The Stress of Life. New York: McGraw-Hill.

SHAFER, E.L. and J. MIETZ (1969) "Aesthetic and emotional experience rates high with northeast wilderness hikers." Environment & Behavior 1: 186-197.

SHAFER, E.L. and R.C. THOMSON (1968) "Models that describe use of Adirondack campgrounds." Forest Sciences 14: 383-391.

SHERROD, D. (1974) "Crowding, perceived contol and behavioral after-effects." Journal of Applied Psychology 4: 171-186.

_____ and R. DOWNS (1974) "Environmental determinants of altruism: the effects of stimulus overload and perceived control on helping." Journal of Experimental Social Psychology 10: 468-479.

SIBONY, A. (1979) Le Bruit à l'Ecole. (unpublished)

SIMMEL, G. (1950) The Sociology of Georg Simmel. New York: Free Press.

SINGER, J. (1978) The need to measure life style." Presented at the symposium on environmental evaluation, 19th International Congress of Psychology.

_____ (n.d.) "Social and sociological impact of transportation noise." (unpublished)

SIVADON, P. and F. GAUTHERET (1965) La Rééducation Corporelle des Fonctions Mentales. Paris: Editions Sociales Françaises.

SIVADON, P., A. BAKER, and R. DAVIES (1960) Psychiatric Services and Architecture. Geneva: Cahiers de Santé Publique.

SOMMER, R. (1974) Tight Spaces. Englewood Cliffs, NJ: Prentice-Hall.

_____ (1970) "The ecology of study areas." Environment & Behavior 2: 271-280.

_____ (1966) "The ecology of privacy." Library Quarterly 36: 234-248.

_____ (1962) "The distances for comfortable conversation: a further study." Sociometry 25: 111-116.

_____ (1959) "Studies in personal space." Sociometry 22: 247-260.

_____ and F. D. BECKER (1969) "Territorial defense and the good neighbor." Journal of Psychiatry and Social Psychology 11: 86-92.

SONNENFELD, J. (1969) "Equivalence and distortion of the perceptual environment." Environment & Behavior 1: 83-99.

_____ (1966) "Variable values in space landscape: an inquiry into the nature of environmental necessity." Journal of Social Issues 27: 71-82.

SPERANDIO, J.C. (1975) "Etude de la signalisation spécifique de la ville nouvelle d'Evry." (unpublished)

SROLE, L. (1972) "Urbanization and mental health: some reformulations." American Scientist 60, 4: 576-583.

STANKEY, G. H. (1972) "A strategy for the definition and management of wilderness qualities," in J. U. Krutilla (ed.) Natural Environments: Studies in Theoretical and Applied Analysis. Baltimore, MD: Johns Hopkins University Press.

STEINZOR, B. (1950) "The spatial factor in face to face discussion groups." Journal of Abnormal Social Psychology 45: 552-555.

STOKOLS, D. (1977) "Origins and directions of environment-behavioral research," ch. 1 in D. Stokols (ed.) Perspectives in Environment and Behavior. New York: Plenum Press.

_____ (1976) "The experience of crowding in primary and secondary environments." Environment & Behavior 8, 1: 49-87.

_____ (1972) "On the distinction between density and crowding: implications for future research." Psychological Review 79, 3: 275-277.

_____ M. RALL, B. PINNER, and J. SCHOPLEN (1973) "Physical, social and personal determinants of the perception of crowding." Environment & Behavior 5, 1: 87-115.

STRINGER, P. (1975) "Understanding the city," in D. Canter (ed.) Environmental Interaction. London: Surrey University Press.

STUDER, R. (1970) "The organization of spatial stimuli," in L. Pastalan, and D. Carson (eds.) The Spatial Behavior of Older People. Ann Arbor: University of Michigan Press.

SUNDSTROM, E. (1973) "An experimental study of crowding." Journal of Personality and Social Psychology 32, 4: 645-654.

_____ and I. ALTMAN (1974) "Field study of dominance and territorial behavior." Journal of Psychiatry and Social Psychology 30, 1: 115-125.

TARRIÉRE, C. (1962) "Les effets non-auditifs du bruit sur le comportement." Bulletin du Centres d'Etudes et de Recherches Psychotechniques 11: 355-378.

TAYLOR, W., J. PEARSON, A. MAIR, and W. BORNS (1965) "Study of noise and hearing in jute weaving." Journal of the Acoustical Society of America 38, 4: 113-122.

THEOLOGUS, G. C., G. R. WHEATON, and E. R. FLEISHMAN (1974) "Effects of intermittent, inordinate intensity noise on human performance." Journal of Applied Psychology 59: 539-547.

TIMMS, D. W. G. (1971) The Urban Mosaic. Cambridge, MA: Harvard University Press.

TOLMAN, E. (1932) Purposive Behavior in Animals and Men. New York: Appleton-Century-Crofts.

_____ and E. BRUNSWIK (1935) "The organism and the causal texture of the environment." Psychological Review 42: 43-77.

TUCKER, L. R. (1978) "The environmentally concerned citizen." Environment & Behavior 10, 3: 389-419.

VALINS, S. and A. BAUM (1973) "Residential group size, social interaction and crowding." Environment & Behavior 5: 421-439.

VURPILLOT, E. (1974) "Début de la construction de l'espace chez l'enfant," in Y. Hatwell (ed.) De l'Espace Corporel a l'Espace Ecologique. Paris: Presses Universitaires de France.

WACHS, T. D., J. C. UZGIRIS, and J. McHUNT (1971) "Cognitive development in infants of different age levels and from different environmental backgrounds." Merrill-Palmer Quarterly of Behavior Development 17: 288-317.

WEINSTEIN, N. D. (1974) "Effects of noise on intellectual performance." Journal of Applied Psychology 59: 548-554.

WELLS, B. W. P. (1965) "The psycho-social influence of building environment: sociometric findings in large and small office spaces." Building Sciences 1: 153-165.

WESTIN, A. F. (1967) Privacy and Freedom. New York: Atheneum.

WHITE, W. P. (1976) Alternate Job Settings in Environment and Behavior. Washington, DC: American Psychological Association.

WICKER, A. (1968) "Undermanning, performance and students' subjective experiences in behavior settings of large and small high schools." Journal of Personality and Social Psychology 10: 255-261.

_____ J. E. McCRATH, and G. ARMSTRONG (1972) "Organization size and behavior setting capacity as determinants of member participation." Behavioral Science 17: 499-513.

WILKINSON, R. T. (1963) "Interaction of noise with knowledge of results and sleep deprivation." Journal of Experimental Psychology 66: 332-337.

WINKEL, G. H. and R. SASANOFF (1976) "An approach to an objective analysis of behavior in architectural space," in H. Proshansky et al. (eds.) Environmental Psychology. New York: Holt, Rinehart & Winston.

WINKEL, G. H., R. MALEK, and P. THIEL (1970) "Community response to the design features of roads: a technique for measurement." Highway Research Record 30: 133-145.

WINSBOROUGH, H. H. (1965) "The social consequences of high population density." Law and Contemporary Problems 30: 120-126.

WITKIN, H. A. (1959) "The perception of the upright." Scientific American 200: 50-56.

WOOD, D. (1971) "Fleeting glimpses: adolescent and other images of the entity called San Christobal las Casas, Chiapas, Mexico." M.A. thesis, Clark University.

WOODHEAD, M. M. (1964) "The effects of bursts of noise on an arithmetic task." American Journal of Psychology 77: 627-633.

WOOLS, R. and D. CANTER (1970) "The effects of the meaning of buildings on behavior." Applied Ergonomics 1: 144-150.

WRIGHT, H. F. (1967) Recording and Analyzing Child Behavior. New York: Harper & Row.

ZANADELLI, H. A. (1969) "Life in a landscape office," in N. Polities (ed.) Improving Office Environment. Elmhurst: Business Press.

ZAVALLONI, M. (1977) Environmental Perception. UNESCO.

ZEHNER, R. B. (1972) "Neighborhood and community satisfaction: a report on new towns and less planned suburbs," in J. F. Wohlwill and D. H. Carson (eds.) Environment and the Social Sciences: Perspectives and Application. Washington, DC: American Psychological Association.

ZEISEL, J. (1971) "Fundamental values in planning with the non-paying client," in C. Burnette (ed.) Architecture for Human Behavior. Philadelphia: American Institute of Architecture.

ZIMBARDO, P. G. (1969) "The human choices: individuation, reason and order versus disindividuation, impulse and chaos," in W. J. Arnold and D. Levine (eds.) Nebraska Symposium on Motivation. Lincoln: University of Nebraska Press.

ZLUTNICK, S. and I. ALTMAN (1972) "Crowding and human behavior," in J. Wohlwill and D. H. Carson (eds.) Environment and the Social Sciences: Perspectives and Application. Washington, DC: American Psychological Association.

About the Author

Claude Levy-Leboyer is currently Vice-President of the Université René Descartes in Paris and President of the Office of Continuing Education at that university. She taught previously at the Universities of Paris and Rouen. Since 1974 she has acted as editor-in-chief of the *International Review of Applied Psychology*. She has published articles in numerous journals, most notably *Le Travail Humain, Année Psychologique*, and the *Bulletin of the International Association of Applied Psychology*. Her most recent books include *Le Psychologue et l'enterprise* (1980) and *Etude psychologique du cadre de vie* (1977).

About the Translators

David Canter is a Reader in Psychology and **Ian Griffiths** a Lecturer in Environmental Psychology. Both teach at the University of Surrey and have published and consulted widely in their technical and professional fields. Both have lectured widely—David Canter in America and the Far East, and Ian Griffiths in Europe, particularly in France where he has also undertaken consultancy assignments.